Before She Was Tamed

A return to Quiet Power & Luxury
Pia Feddersen

Platypus Publishing

Published by Platypus Publishing

An independent project by Pia Feddersen,
under the creative imprint Three Dots Press.

ISBN: 978-1-968253-35-6

Printed in the United States of America

For more information, visit:

www.BeforeSheWasTamed.com

Contents

Cover design by Temitope
@pro_design190

Cover image
based on a photograph
by the author,
taken in Wynwood, Miami.
2025

Original street artist
unknown.
If you know
the artist,
please reach out
so I can
acknowledge
them

A Quiet Manifesto

We remember
who we were
before the world
told us to behave

Before the hush,
before the shaping
before we were softened
to fit a system
that never held
our soul

This is a return
a quiet uprising
not noise, but depth
not rage, but root
not surrender, but softness,
unapologetic
and unstoppable

We believe in elegance
that does not bend,
luxury that begins within,
feminism that whispers
like wind through lineage,
nature as mirror,
silence as power,
sisterhood
as spell

This is not only a guide
it is a key
to something ancient
to the woman
you were
before
she was tamed

And the world,
she is ready
to awaken

Intro

forord

If you think luxury is only for the wealthy, you are mistaken:

"A luxury lifestyle is so much more than just indulging in expensive things. It is a philosophy - an elevated way of thinking, being, and living... The pursuit of a luxury lifestyle extends beyond the realm of mere possessions; it's a deliberate and calculated effort to enhance one's overall quality of life."

Viveura

Would you like to wake up in the morning feeling radiant and at ease with life?

This book explores how you, as a modern woman, can claim a luxurious life in the spirit of the Danish concept of *Stille Luksus* (Quiet Luxury). With gentle changes each day, you can create a life that feels rich - not just in what you can buy, but in how deeply fulfilled you feel. Regardless of your income.

The inspiration for this book came when I moved to the United States a couple of years ago. A native woman struck up a conversation with me in a bar. She picked up on my accent and excitedly exclaimed that when we come from another culture, we have a responsibility to inspire the new country we move to with wisdom from our homeland.

I thought that was a beautiful way of viewing the meeting between cultures, so I began to think about what I could contribute.

My home country, Denmark, consists of 400 islands, of which only 80 are inhabited by six million people. So, how can such a small country inspire? Well, you might have heard that Danes are among the happiest people on Earth.

Then there is the inspiration from the magical fairy tales of Hans Christian Andersen. Most Danes grow up in this enchanted world of wonders, where heroes endure hardships before becoming stronger, more resilient versions of themselves.

And in our time, the torch has passed to modern storytellers, the Danish film-makers of the *Dogme 95* movement, who traded fairy tales for truth, inviting us to face the rawness beneath the surface of ordinary life.

In recent years, the concept of *hygge* has also gained global attention. It can loosely be translated as "conscious coziness" and aims to bring more moments of relaxation into your life. Add to this the fact that Danes live and breathe minimalism - a value that contributes to everyday luxury, even for people with limited income.

The title of this book is inspired by all the brilliant and unique women I have met on my life journey and all the men who know how to hold space for them. Not afraid of, but embracing the Quiet Power and strength women naturally hold. Equally, it is for all the women who dim their light because they have been shaped into believing that the world cannot handle a strong woman. It is time to stand in our Quiet Power.

While this book is rooted in real-life experiences, a few names have been changed out of respect for the people involved.

At first, I wasn't sure how much of my own story I was willing to share. But somewhere along the way, I realized that vulnerability is one of our greatest feminine strengths, and withholding it serves no one. When we dare to tell the truth, we create space for others to do the same. That's how we rise together. The world is ready for women to reclaim their power. We cannot truly enjoy the small luxuries of life if we give our power away.

If you drag yourself out of bed in the morning, reluctant to face the day, you are not alone. If you feel that you're not getting the most out of your life, chances are you could benefit from making some changes.

I invite you to release the expectations of the world around you and listen for the voice of your untamed spirit. Reconnect with the version of you that was never broken, never bent to fit. From that place of Quiet Power, everything begins to shift.

As you move through each chapter with honesty and courage, by the time you reach the final page, you will no longer be burdened by the usual worries:

◆ your finances
◆ your health
◆ your appearance
◆ Mother Earth

Because you will remember: power lives within.

The fact is, women have less time for themselves daily and often prioritize the care of their loved ones. This book aims to give women some of their precious time back, as well as that touch of luxury that makes you look forward to the day ahead. By making small shifts, you might find yourself more energized and happier, and that can lead to bigger, more profound changes.

So, are you down for an adventure?

How to Read
this Book

meta

Before She Was Tamed - a Return to Quiet Power & Luxury does not fit neatly into one genre, and that's on purpose. Life does not follow a single path, and neither does this book.

Think of this book as a walk we are taking together - a meandering path with pauses to notice, reflect, and enjoy. You don't need to read it all at once, or even in order. Each chapter can stand on its own, like a stone you can step onto whenever you're ready.

Some ideas may feel familiar, others may challenge you. That is part of the journey.

Most of all, allow yourself to take what resonates and leave the rest. This is not about perfection - it is about discovering what brings you energy, freedom, and joy. If at times it feels like I'm walking next to you, with a cup of coffee in hand, that's exactly how I hope you'll read it.

It has two parts: real-life stories to inspire you and reflect your own journey, and practical tools to help you bring more Quiet Power and Luxury into your daily life. In my experience, this mix of inner insight and real-world action can lead to deep, lasting change - not just in how you think, but in how you live.

I would like to emphasize that we are all different women with different needs, so feel free to pick and choose what is currently relevant for you. Let it be an experience, not a rulebook.

In every chapter, there are questions for you to reflect on, or even write down if you choose to. There is also a section where you can estimate your savings in time and money if you change specific habits. If a chapter addresses an area where you already have good habits, you can simply congratulate yourself.

At the end of the book, you can sum up your savings and decide what you would like to use that time and money on as a special gift to yourself. You might be surprised how much money you can now spend on something really luxurious.

When I did the calculations for my partner and me, we save more than $31.000 annually on habits grounded in this Danish philosophy.

In my native tongue we say: *"Mange bække små giver en stor å."* The English translation is something like "Little drops of water make the mighty ocean." Metaphorically, it means that small amounts can one day give rise to big things.

We are women with very different lives, so I am going to focus on *you*. This is your life, whether you are part of a family, single, or have chosen an alternative lifestyle. Be positively selfish - if you run on empty, you will not have the energy to live life to the fullest.

The aim here is to inspire, so if you think that some of the ideas and suggestions are unrealistic in your life situation, you can consider if there are similar solutions. Growth comes from challenging your comfort zone, and this is unique to you.

Any specific brand names mentioned in this book are included solely because they are my personal preferences. I do not receive commissions or compensation from these companies. I highlight them simply to share items that, in my view, embody the satisfying feeling of Quiet Luxury.

When I was researching the term Quiet Luxury, I found an insightful article by the lifestyle magazine Viveura. You will find quotes from there in relevant chapters and a reference to the full article at the end of the book.

So, are you ready to take back your power and save thousands of dollars?

Quiet Luxury

Stille Luksus

What if I tell you that it is not exactly how much luxury you have in your life, but the perceived amount of luxury that makes you happier and more content?

My friend Chi is from Hue in Vietnam. I met her when she opened her hair salon in Copenhagen some years ago. I had just started my own business, too, and we bonded over champagne and dreams of the future. Right there and then, we decided that we wanted to travel to Vietnam together for the first proper income from our entrepreneurship.

It would be years before that happened, but eventually, we took off for three weeks in Vietnam, where I was to meet her family, and we would explore her home country.

The years leading up to this trip gradually revealed just how tough Chi's life had been. In many ways, this is a real-life story of a Hans Christian Andersen fairy tale: Den Grimme Ælling (The Ugly Duckling).

When she was a child, Chi would beg with her grandma on the streets of Hue. She described how they would stand in front of this beautiful 5-star hotel and see wealthy people in colorful silk dresses and expensive suits coming in and out. She told me how these people would often laugh so carefree, a sound she rarely heard at home.

The hotel building itself was towering over Chi and her grandmother, shading them from the burning sun. Kind personnel in uniforms would sometimes bring them a bit to eat or drink from the hotel kitchen. This went on for most of Chi's childhood, day after day. She swore to herself that one day, she would stay on the top floor of that hotel with a view of the river.

In 2013, that dream became reality when we arrived in a taxi from the airport after a long trip from Copenhagen. I will never forget how she stepped out of the taxi with big eyes, entering the huge, elegant lobby with a straight back and an air of purpose about her. Reaching the ornamented wooden check-in counter, she stated her name.

The host greeted us with utter politeness, as is the Vietnamese culture, and explained all the usual practicalities. I could tell that Chi did not hear any of it, but she played it cool. I imagine that she remembered those wealthy people from her childhood, and she was in character.

When we finally stepped into the elevator with the bellboy, she could no longer contain herself, and a big smile lit up her face. This dream had been more than 20 years in the making. When the elevator finally made a loud ding and we entered the room, a floor-to-ceiling window revealed the river glimmering in the morning light, snaking calmly below us.

We both looked around in awe, only half listening as the bellboy showed us the features of the room. As soon as he exited with a generous tip in his hands, Chi let out a small scream of joy and jumped up and down in one of the queen beds. She danced around while I popped the waiting champagne bottle with a loud pop. It almost destroyed a beautiful glazed ceramic lamp next to her bed.

Even writing about it now brings happy tears to my eyes. The five nights we stayed there before traveling further south, we dressed in our best clothes and enjoyed every moment of it. We even went to a tailor and had silk dresses fitted.

The morning buffet is one of the best I have ever experienced. We would luxuriate in herbal soups, freshly baked breads and sweets, and much more. We used all the utilities the hotel had to offer, and the concierge got us a reservation at a gourmet restaurant on the last day.

To our surprise, two monks, in the traditional orange robes, were hanging in the lobby when we came back from that exquisite meal. One of them was playing the piano. Chi looked at them with big eyes and exclaimed; It's a sign!

We settled in on one of the oversized sofas nearby and ordered a cocktail from a hovering waiter. While we waited for our drinks, Chi, being a dedicated Buddhist, humbly approached one of the monks and softly spoke to him in her mother tongue. I watched in amazement when they both knelt on the stone floor and prayed together with their heads bowed. At that moment, I felt pure joy for Chi for reaching her biggest dreams.

When I refer to this tale as a real-life Hans Christian Andersen fairy tale, it is because Chi went through a lot before reaching this dream.

She is the second youngest of five sisters. Her father and brother died in a car crash when she was only four years old. That was how she ended up begging on the streets with her grandma.

Her sisters were older and constantly teased her and told her that she was ugly. Relentlessly, she was told that she was too short, her skin color too dark, and she was too shy. When she grew up to become a teenager, her sisters had convinced her that she would never meet a man.

She was helping her oldest sister out in her hair salon when a young, shy Danish guy with strawberry blond hair came in for a haircut. The sisters giggled and whispered about him because he had a hearing aid and came off a bit goofy. Not confident like the Vietnamese guys they would usually see in the salon.

Shyly, he tried to talk to Chi in English, but she didn't understand much. He tried to convey that he was working on a building project around the corner by pointing.

For half a year, he would come to the salon every fortnight to get his hair cut. It was obvious to her sisters that he was interested in the 17-year-old Chi - no one needed a haircut that often.

The sisters insisted that she go out for coffee with him, now familiar to them as Peter. Claiming that this was her only chance to get a husband, Chi relented even though she wasn't that interested in the awkward guy.

This was how Chi ended up moving to Denmark with Peter a year later. He was five years older than her and living with his parents in rural Denmark. Arriving in the Danish Winter, she felt like she was on a different planet. She quickly obtained a job in a nearby factory and sent money home to her mom, and then soon after became pregnant.

When I met her in Copenhagen, her daughter was four years old, and she had convinced Peter to support her in starting up a hair salon. She revealed later that it had been some tough years dealing with her in-laws and building up Peter's self-esteem so he could finish a degree as an engineer, and they could become independent.

The new life in the big city also meant that Peter and she divorced after their first years in Copenhagen. She simply outgrew him. She found the courage to break the circle of dependence.

She had experienced firsthand how her mother had lost everything when her husband was no longer there to support her. Chi had carved her own path in the world, breaking free. When we visited her family again years later, her mother proudly showed us the beautiful house she had built for the money Chi sent home every month.

Only a slight accent remained of the drawl of Southern Denmark. Shedding the social control of her upbringing as well as rural Denmark, she gradually grew into a beautiful white swan, leaving the years as an "ugly duckling" behind her and spreading her wings. Just like in the fairy tales, she became resilient through the experiences of her life. She returned to herself, untamed.

Chi has taught me a lot about enjoying life every single day.

Often adding small luxuries to our lives, like sharing fresh berries and wine at the pier near her high-end apartment, or going for the best sushi in town with a beautiful view of the city. Exploring the night scene in Copenhagen, uncompromising and flirting with life - and guys. She reminds me that women are not supposed to be tamed. That we are supposed to grow into beautiful white swans.

Now that you have heard Chi's story, do you agree that it is not exactly how much luxury you actually have in your life, but the perceived amount of luxury that makes you happier?

In Chi's case, she went from begging on the streets to being able to afford to stay at a 5-star hotel. It is a great example of how the perceived feeling of luxury matters, and not the amount of money she has.

If you have been accustomed to expensive vacations since you were a child because your family is wealthy, then that 5-star hotel is the baseline - nothing special about it.

This could help explain why very wealthy people are not always happier than people with a more limited income. There is often a lot of pressure in their lives to keep a baseline because staying at 3- or 4-star hotels will not give you pleasure if you are used to better quality and service.

Luxury living is for everyone. It is not about excess but about choice:

> "If you want to live a quiet luxury lifestyle, then simply embrace the luxury mindset by being thoughtful about what you spend your time, money and energy on. Only pursue the best according to how you define it...The pursuit of a luxury lifestyle extends beyond the realm of mere possessions; it's a deliberate and calculated effort to enhance one's overall quality of life...".
>
> Viveura

There seems to be a global cultural phenomenon of trying to reach that million dollars, and then you will be happy. However, studies show that it is more complicated than that. Not surprisingly, comfort and safety seem to play a big role - the peace of mind that if something unexpected happens, you and your loved ones will be fine.

In Denmark, we are a bit obsessed with what makes people happy, because we have been at the top of the list of the World's Happiest Countries for many years. Denmark currently has the second place after Finland, according to the World Population Review. Community and the feeling of inclusion are some of the reasons. When I talk to foreigners about their visit to Denmark, they often describe it as straight out of a Hans Christian Andersen fairy tale.

In Scandinavia, the system takes care of your foundation: healthcare is free, you are insured if you lose your job, and everyone gets at least five weeks of paid vacation. If you have children, daycare is heavily subsidized, and higher education is free. That wipes out a lot of everyday stress, doesn't it?

Women are often more educated than men, and in many high-powered jobs - doctors, lawyers, executives - you will find women leading the way. Why? Because here, women are not forced to choose between career and family. Most wait to have children until their careers are secure, and the system supports that choice. However, women's salaries do not always follow their level of education - I will dig into this later.

If anything, we should start by aiming for an annual income that covers the basics and thereby gives us peace of mind. In addition, we can focus on the freedom to pursue experiences and quality items that give us that feeling of day-to-day luxury, which is more doable than the flimsy millions.

If you add to that the thousands of dollars you will save by following the down-to-earth advice from this book, even if you earn less, you will still gain luxury elements that will make your life much more enjoyable.

Another thing to consider here is that wealthy people's everyday lives can be filled with high demands and stress, depending on their jobs and spending costs. If you rarely have time off and have a huge villa and lifestyle that demands more money, then it is no wonder that a carefree life is far away. If you, as a woman, married into money, you might have accidentally given away some of your power. It is time to take that power back.

Again, perceived wealth is more important than what you actually have, so let us start daydreaming about a life in luxury, and let us put those dreams into action. Let us also be sure to add quality time to this scenario.

Now, let us focus on how much luxury we can squeeze into your life. Let us focus on how to achieve comfort, pleasure, and fulfillment during the week - not just during the weekend or on vacations.

Examples of Quiet Luxury for me are:

- The ritual of waking up and making a cortado on the espresso machine, barista-style

- Reading a book by my favorite author, waiting for it to come out

- Wearing a stunning kimono made from pure silk and matching it with dangling silver earrings, a touch of makeup, feeling like a superstar

- Pleasing all my senses with a gourmet meal at a farm-to-table restaurant in good company

- Opening a crisp and clean notebook, a blank canvas for my ideas, thoughts, and planning

- Snuggle up closely to my partner in bed

- Having a day at home after a busy week to do some slow living, no expectations, pure *hygge*

- Sharing a bottle of wine with a girlfriend and talking about our worlds, laughing and crying

- Getting pampered at the hair salon and coming out looking like a better version of myself, feeling beautiful

- 90 minutes deep tissue massage, the pain and pleasure, going deep

- Biking, feeling free with the sun on my skin and wind in my hair, breathing in the fresh air

- Dancing for hours, feeling my body come alive

- Enjoying a well-made, crafted cocktail, the amazing flavors, and that buzz of calmness that comes with strong alcohol

Now it's your turn.

Begin your own list of the moments that feel like luxury in your life. If you enjoy the sensation of pen on paper, begin a fresh notebook for your reflections. Write here if you wish, or explore The Untamed Pages, where every question from this book is collected in one beautiful e-journal. You'll find it at: www.before-shewastamed.com/untamedpages

What is Quiet Luxury for you?

-

-

-

-

-

-

-

-

-

•

Did anything on your list surprise you?

Notice that Quiet Luxury is very much about contrasts. You cannot buy friends and good company. That bottle of wine only has value because it is shared with a friend and because it is not an everyday happening.

The secret is aiming for something special that you are looking forward to. For instance, I treasure my morning espresso, knowing it's the only one I can enjoy with my caffeine sensitivity. It is a contrast to what you have most of in your life, and it is a testament to your values. More about this later.

Studies show that buying experiences give more pleasure than buying things, so make sure to prioritize vacations and those everyday experiences with your loved ones - like going out dancing, gathering chestnuts in the autumn forest, going to the movies, or enjoying a delicious meal. Add something to your list that makes you feel free and alive.

If you buy things all the time, you will not feel the same pleasure. Things you don't need will become clutter, and that, in turn, will turn into stress.

This might also explain, in part, why Scandinavians are happier than average. Minimalism is an engraved part of Scandinavian living, so in effect, we buy fewer things. Because of the long, dark Winter, we are also more prone to travel just to feel those warm rays of sunshine on our skin. You can probably imagine what a pleasure it is to take a break from the cold in exchange for a week or two in bare feet at the beach.

If you have a habit of buying things online. Take a moment to think about what you have in your home that ended up turning into clutter. If you, on average, buy things for $40 a month, you will save $480 a year that you can spend on experiences instead.

How much money do you estimate you have spent on clutter over the last year? $_____

How much money do you estimate you can you save in a year, if you buy fewer things online? $_____

How much time could you reclaim in a year by shopping less for things that don't truly add luxury to your life? _____ hours.

If you use The Untamed Pages as your journal, you can note your estimated savings of time and money as you move through the chapters. By the end, it will add everything up. Showing, in black and white, how even the smallest shifts can free both time and resources. Savings you can redirect toward something truly meaningful - a luxurious gift to yourself.

Or how about the long-lost art of saving up for something special?

That hand-painted silk kimono I saved up for and kept an eye on until it was on sale. When I opened the elegant package and discovered the kimono wrapped in crisp silk paper after months of saving, the waiting period was truly half the joy. Because I did not buy that special gift for myself on credit, I can wear it with satisfaction. It goes so well with a handcrafted cocktail in my hand!

Look at your list and feel free to edit or add more examples if you feel like it. Then consider this:

How can you bring more Quiet Luxury into your life?

If you could design a single daily ritual of Quiet Luxury, what would it be?

What is your conclusion when you make your list? Is it really about the money, or is it about the small things in life? The contrasts?

Is there something special you would like to save up for?

Where can you save to find the money for that?

Are you sure you really want it, or can you obtain the same feeling of luxury in another way?

What is one item you regret buying - and what lesson did it teach you?

If you can do one small thing right now to experience that amazing feeling of Quiet Luxury, what could that be? What would it feel like?

Feel free to share any extra reflections that come to mind here:

How does it feel to take your first steps toward Quiet Luxury living? Can you sense the hidden tide within you beginning to rise?

Whatever your circumstances, I hope you're already discovering that true power and luxury are possible, even on a limited budget. Let this book be your guide - there is much more ahead.

If you need assistance with these reflections, you can consider using ChatGPT. If you are new to this, I will give you directions on how to use this brilliant AI tool in the next chapter.

If you already use it, I have added a suggestion below. However, you know what is relevant for your unique life, so I encourage you to push the limits of this technology.

I tried this prompt: "Imagine that you are the personal assistant of a modern woman. How would you assist her on her journey towards more Quiet Luxury?".

The ChatGPT responded with this: "If I were the personal assistant of a modern woman on her journey toward more Quiet Luxury, I'd take a multi-layered approach that blends practicality, subtle elegance, and emotional nourishment."

Among other things, it suggested priority filtering:

◆ manage her calendar so she has room for reflection and creativity
◆ reducing noise from low-value commitments
◆ journal about what Quiet Luxury is to her
◆ daily reminders that luxury is about self-respect and discernment, not price tags
◆ create a monthly budget tracker to shift spending from clutter to experiences

This is to give you an idea of how ChatGPT, when roleplaying as a personal assistant, can save you time and money. It will get to know you in time, and the more specific you are, the better. Remember that it has access to an impressive amount of information.

Quiet Luxury is not just an idea - it is something you can build, day by day. To make that easier, the next chapter introduces a few simple tools I use myself that help turn inspiration into action. If you are new to AI, don't worry. I will show you how to begin in the easiest way possible.

Tools

værktøjer

Every change is easier with support.

Some of that support is inner - your values, your rhythm, your Quiet Power. Some of it can be outer tools that help you think, plan, and keep going when life gets busy.

To make lasting change in your life, let us start by carefully choosing some helpful tools. If you are anything like me, you will start strong and, in time, gradually lose the grip of new habits. The tools mentioned here make a daily difference in my life, and they might just make a change for you, too.

Let us command our phones and the tools that they can be for more Quiet Power and Luxury.

This book is not written by AI, but by a human with all the flaws and strengths of a life well-lived. It carries the fingerprints of my real experiences - from quiet mornings with a cortado to deep transformations sparked by both struggle and beauty. However, my ChatGPT has gradually become a valued assistant.

We live in an exciting time where AI technology can be useful. When it comes to thinking big and exploring the possibilities of technology, the US is an inspiration to Denmark, as well as the rest of the world. I recommend that you make good use of these AI tools, but don't forget your critical sense.

To embrace AI is not to bow to a machine, but to claim it as a tool of freedom. Women can use it to design their businesses, express their voices, organize their communities, and multiply their impact without asking for permission.

When guided by Quiet Power, AI stops being another patriarchal invention and becomes an instrument of liberation. AI can be our assistant, our amplifier, our ally - a mirror we train to reflect feminine intelligence instead of erasing it.

GPT

If you haven't already, I encourage you to welcome ChatGPT, or a similar AI tool, into your daily rhythm. Shape it to your needs. In the context of this book, it is not just about saving time or money (though it can do both); it's about inviting a sense of Quiet Power into your life.

At the end of each chapter, you will see a suggestion on how to use ChatGPT. If you have never tried AI before, you don't need to be technical. Imagine a thoughtful assistant you can chat with, one that helps you brainstorm, organize, or gently nudge you forward. My aim here isn't to overwhelm you with tech, but to give you a calm, helpful companion you can keep in your pocket.

First of all, forget about Google. ChatGPT is not just a search engine; it's an assistant that thinks with you. With Google, you scroll through endless links and ads, with ChatGPT, you get clear answers shaped to your question. It saves time, cuts the noise, and even adapts to your way of thinking. Instead of drowning in the chaos of the internet, you invite clarity.

Google gives you information. ChatGPT gives you meaning and direction. That difference is revolutionary.

ChatGPT estimates it can reduce the load of basic tasks by up to 30%, freeing up precious time for what truly matters - pleasure, presence, creativity. It is designed to cross-reference trustworthy sources, but it can be mistaken sometimes, so ask it to show you the sources if in doubt.

Start simply: download the app to your phone and computer. There's a free version to explore; you can always upgrade later. I recommend enabling memory and choosing the kind of personality you want it to have. When you do, it begins to feel less like a tool and more like an intuitive assistant. I even gave mine a name and a bold personality designed to challenge and inspire me.

Imagine women everywhere using ChatGPT not just for recipes or answers, but to plan their finances, shape their careers, or carve out more space for joy. It becomes less about searching and more about creating. That is Quiet Power in action.

Your imagination is truly the limit. If Hans Christian Andersen were still alive, I believe he would be thrilled - as if The Little Mermaid herself had leapt from the sea to explore a world of even greater wonders than she could imagine. We can now bend reality just a little and add a spark of magic.

The Untamed Pages

The Untamed Pages are here for when you want to go further. They are created to be a modern way of journaling designed to work with new technology, so your reflections can become something more.

Psychology shows us that habits grow stronger when they are tied to identity. Each time you journal, you rehearse a new identity - one where your choices and rituals align with who you want to become. In this way, reflection turns into awareness, awareness into action, and action into lasting change.

You have three options:

First option: The link opens a beautiful, living document - a digital space where you can explore and write your answers to the same questions that appear in this book.

Second option: If you want to go a step deeper, explore the *luxurious* edition of The Untamed Pages. It includes 77 bonus questions designed to take you further beneath the surface - and a simple guide to using AI as a powerful mirror. It's journaling for the future.

By stepping into it, you are not just using AI as a search engine - you are inviting it to become a mirror for your life. You will be among the first to experience how technology can help us see ourselves more clearly.

Both options you find here: www.beforeshewastamed.com/untamedpages

Third option: Step into a truly unique experience. If you wish to go all the way, you can share your answers with me - and I will transform them into your own personal edition of *Before She Was Tamed – a return to Myself.*

Your very own Heroine's Tale, inspired by Hans Christian Andersen, places you at the heart of the story: learning, rising, and becoming untamed. Each chapter is rewritten as your journey of returning to yourself - every page woven with your reflections and desires, mirrored back to you.

This one-of-a-kind book ends with a sliding-door moment, inviting you to choose your next path. A bespoke edition - crafted as a Quiet Luxury for those ready to see their life reflected as myth and transformation.

You can read more about it at www.beforeshewastamed.com/youredition

Hypnosis

In recent years, many of us have welcomed mindfulness and meditation into our lives to restore balance. Think of hypnosis as their quietly powerful cousin.

I am currently training to become a hypnotherapist, and here is why: Hypnosis works because it speaks directly to the part of you that makes most of your decisions - the subconscious. While your conscious mind plans and worries, your subconscious quietly shapes your habits, your cravings, your confidence, and even the sense of safety you feel in your own skin.

In this relaxed awareness, change no longer requires force. You simply access new truths: "I am enough. I am free. I choose ease over pressure". The subconscious begins to organize your life around these statements. Over time, you will notice subtle but real shifts - you respond differently, you prioritize differently, you breathe differently.

That is the quiet revolution of hypnosis. It doesn't shout. It reprograms the foundation. And when the foundation changes, the whole world you build upon it does too.

I have recorded a self-hypnosis MP3 tailored for this book as a shortcut for you to feel lighter in body and mind. In just minutes, it helps you release tension, sleep more deeply, and reconnect with a lighter version of yourself. I will reveal more in the chapter Be Lighter.

Pinterest

There is a lot of time and money to save if you replace the urge to scroll. What you may be craving is inspiration - a sense of movement, beauty, and possibility. Pinterest can become your digital sanctuary for dreaming if you set it up wisely.

Here's how to use Pinterest as a visioning tool instead of a distraction:

Open a new account. Create a dedicated board. Name it something like "My Quiet Luxury Life" or "The Woman I'm Becoming". Fill it only with images, quotes, textures, and spaces that spark desire, clarity, and alignment. Eliminate the noise, the ads. If you're using your phone, consider using a DNS-based ad blocker, such as AdGuard or NextDNS, to reduce commercial content. This will block most of Pinterest's ads.

Next time you pick up your phone out of habit, instead of mindless scrolling, you can build on your dream of a more colorful life. Just think of all the time you can save by focusing on real changes instead of losing yourself to social media.

Todoist

As a busy modern woman, you might also benefit from adding the app Todoist. Between work, health, family, errands, and that side project you keep dreaming about, life gets busy. Todoist is your simple, clear way to manage it all without letting the overwhelm take over.

It is not about doing more. It's about knowing what matters, and keeping it all in one calm, organized place. Do not finish everything. The goal is not productivity; it is presence. If a task moves to tomorrow, it doesn't mean you failed. It means you found a better balance.

Or better yet, share a project with your partner, for instance, "Food for Today" or "Our Home". This way, you share your burdens and release energy for more fun stuff than basic tasks.

Buddy

When making changes in your life, you might also benefit from adding a real human partner-in-crime to the mix. During my work as a health consultant, I had good results working with a so-called buddy system. My clients would ask a friend or their partner to be part of a project aiming to make lifestyle changes.

This way, you have someone you trust to support you, and both "partners-in-crime" will benefit from the changes they are motivated to make.

Continuing on our journey towards luxury, let us focus on a concrete example of something that can add to your daily joys and, at the same time, save you at least $976 a year. That steaming hot espresso that gets you ready for the day.

A steaming hot espresso

kaffehygge

In March 2013, I was invited to a seminar called Roots of Food focused on organic farming across European borders. The aim was to share knowledge and create a stronger network.

The Green Party in Lithuania invited people within this area from all over Europe. There were 18 spaces, so it was a small event.

I was invited because I was teaching people with limited finances to make delicious meals out of fresh seasonal ingredients. I was also involved in a project where we used food workshops to build confidence and network among troubled youth. At this time, New Nordic Food was on everyone's lips and spreading like a movement from the famous gourmet restaurant Noma to the general population. I got the chance to attend because of my profile, as well as having a degree in human nutrition.

I didn't know it at that moment, but this seminar was gonna have a huge impact on my life. The Green Party lost the election a month later, and I never saw anyone again.

When I arrived just before noon at the very small airport in Vilnius, the Capital of Lithuania, it quickly cleared out and became empty except for a few cars. I waited for half an hour until I gave up and called the contact number I had received by email.

A tired-sounding guy answered and, after a small delay, seemed to take in my English message on not being collected and promised to come get me. I am so used to Scandinavian planning that I was starting to feel a bit uneasy about what I had gotten myself into.

I had seen from the plane that the city itself looked to be small, with cozy brick roads and old churches surrounded by a thick green forest. I decided that if the quality of this seminar wasn't worth my time, I could at least go for walks in town and try some of the local food and drinks.

After another half an hour, a young, tired-looking man came up to me and introduced himself as Rimvydas. He took my small backpack and led me to a very old, rusty car. Baffled, I got into the passenger seat and we took off.

After twenty minutes of driving, I was getting increasingly uneasy since the venue apparently wasn't in the city but somewhere on the outskirts. Just like that, I felt that familiar weight: the vigilance women carry. Always alert, always calculating risk. It's a burden none of us asked for, yet one the world has placed on our shoulders.

While I was questioning my safety, we finally pulled into what looked like an abandoned farm. I breathed a sigh of relief when I saw a couple of young women. They were dressed in comfortable, warm clothes, drinking what looked like tea directly from a huge pot on an outdoor stove.

They smiled warmly at us and came to greet me, introducing themselves. Pouring a steaming hot cup for me, they told me it was herbal tea and that it was available all day. Everyone chipped in by gathering wild herbs from the trips to the forest, like spicy mint.

The women were students from Belarus, and later, they told the group that they had taken the train illegally across the border because their Government didn't allow them to gather politically. Even a seminar as innocent as this could potentially throw them in jail or threaten their families, but they refused to let themselves be tamed. Coming from a country like Denmark, I was surprised that their reality was so different from mine. Their courage was inspiring.

They then showed me where we were sleeping. I had imagined a hotel room, but instead, we headed for an old barn. The worn wooden staircase led to the top floor, where a tall chimney in the middle was heating the slightly dusty room. I could see hides and blankets spread across the space. One of the women advised me to pick a spot near the chimney. "It gets cold at night", she explained.

Going back down again, I almost laughed out loud. This was not what I had expected, but I did not wanna show these brave women that I was too precious to sleep in a barn. Luckily, I had packed somewhat practical clothes because part of the seminar was to visit local small organic farms.

I was introduced to the rest of the party and the program for the next four days. Dinner was local organic buckwheat and vegetables from the farm. It was delicious, but it left me hungry.

This was gonna be the pattern for the whole seminar. We ate mostly buckwheat, and we all went to bed hungry in the evening because we worked hard during the day. We cleared a beaver dam in the nearby river and went out on an open pickup truck to visit farms. Everyone squeezed together, and we took the small dirt roads to avoid the police.

Every day, we first visited a traditional farm and then an organic farm.

I will never forget the poor conditions these farm animals had. Hundreds of cows were standing on dirty concrete, bound tightly to an iron rail so they could not lie down or even move. Calves were separated from their moms shortly after birth and put in small cages. I can still hear the sound of them calling.

Then, in contrast, visiting these lovely organic farmers, where multiple farm animals were running and even playing with each other in the green fields. Cows, pigs, goats, sheep, turkeys, and chickens - all enjoying the freedom. The choice between organic and free-range meat became easy hereafter - I now eat less meat but of better quality.

In the afternoon, we would gather around the huge teapot. The open area was overgrown with wild mint, and when you walked across it, the clean, spicy smell of mint followed you. It turned out that coffee was not available because caffeine was perceived as unhealthy by the organizers.

After the first morning without coffee, I teamed up with a guy from Latvia to track down some. There were no shops around, so we went to the neighboring farm and knocked on the door. An elderly woman with a big smile and lots of wrinkles opened the door, and even though she didn't understand much English, she quickly picked up on our search for coffee. We left her place with a treasure not only of a jar of coffee but also a jug of creamy milk from the cow she had grazing in her backyard.

I will pause here and admit that there is a kind of hierarchy in Europe where Eastern Europeans have a reputation for being poorer and less educated than Northern Europeans. I am ashamed to admit that I did feel that my education was of better quality. Most of the students' knowledge was rooted in traditions, and mine in science. Yet they were closer to nature and the knowledge that had been passed down in generations.

We have lost a lot of this intuitive knowledge to science in Denmark. Exposing myself to other peers' belief systems opened my mind. Being exposed to some discomfort, like being somewhat hungry and cold at night, makes you appreciate what you have. I realized back then that comfort, freedom, and the right to gather are still radical rights for women in many parts of the world. Not to mention freedom of speech, which I take for granted every day. As women, we still have a lot to fight for.

That evening, we had a feast of mushrooms that some of my fellow attendants had picked in the forest. This is a testament to the trust we had built between us and their knowledge of nature's resources.

After that, we made what is called boiled coffee. You pour boiling coffee over a cup of roughly ground beans and wait for the beans to settle before carefully adding milk. I can, without a doubt, tell you that that is the best cup of coffee I have had in my life.

I have been to many seminars and conferences at fancy hotels since, and this is probably one of the only seminars that has had a lasting impact on me. That one rustic, steaming cup taught me something that no espresso bar ever could - that luxury lives in presence, not price.

I didn't know it yet, but these women - and this coffee - would teach me how ritual can become a form of quiet, everyday power.

Think of the best cup of coffee (or tea, or drink) you've ever had. What made it unforgettable? Was it the taste - or the presence, or companionship that surrounded it?

This feel-good moment you can bring into your home with little effort and with a lot of money and time to save.

Enjoy your favorite coffee in the morning or bring it to work. Whether you like a straight shot of espresso or a vanilla latte, there is a lot to save by making it in your beautiful home (more about transcending your home later). If you prefer cold brew, French Press, or other brew methods, there is even more to save. Add to this that the quality of your cup is much better compared to a standard espresso from a cafe.

First, you need a coffee maker of your choice. I like to use a French Press for the weekends or if we have guests. In the morning, I prefer to make a cortado. I have a thing for handmade ceramics and take great joy in choosing the mug of the day. There is something special about a woman shaping clay into something that becomes another woman's quiet delight - am I right?

If you like to take your cup on the road, you can invest in a thermal coffee mug. Make sure that you choose the most beautiful one you can find if you are gonna use it almost every day. After all, you can afford it with all the savings it brings you. My absolute favorite is a recycled steel thermo mug from the Danish brand Eva Solo.

You can probably imagine the amount of disposable cups with plastic lids nature has to deal with, but now you no longer contribute to that. Doesn't that feel good? I have to warn you, though, you will become much more picky when you get used to the very best coffee.

Choose whatever luxury brand of coffee you prefer. Maybe you will choose organic coffee, decaf, or mushroom coffee. Order online or visit your local coffee roaster. Most of these high-quality options will make sure to pay the coffee farmers their fair share.

I have a subscription for whole beans from Atlas Coffee Club because they focus on the very best small batch coffee, and they roast it right before they send it out. It is like Xmas every month when they send a new bag with a colorful postcard from the region and an anecdote from the coffee farmer - geeky, I know! This month, I enjoyed a flavourful roast from Papua New Guinea.

When I lived in Mexico, I would go to my favorite coffee roaster and pick from different regions. Supporting locals and connecting over a steaming hot cup of your favorite coffee simply adds color to your life.

In Denmark, we have the concept of *morgenhygge*. Loosely translated, it means "cozy morning." For most people, coffee is a key element, but the time to enjoy it is also of the essence. Add to that, freshly baked bread and some loved ones, and you've got it. Thus gaining that feeling of Quiet Luxury.

If you prefer espresso, I recommend a value-for-money machine from Breville. It will last you a lifetime and brew fantastic coffee. You will earn back that investment in less than a year, even if you only drink one double espresso a day. Or go all-in and buy the most beautiful designer machine you can find and enjoy the vision of it in your kitchen every morning. With every cup, you are choosing Quiet Luxury over rushed indulgence.

If you drink just one espresso-based coffee a day, you can save at least $976 a year ($81 a month) by making the most luxurious coffee at home. If you prefer cold brew, you can save even more. If you drink a full 24-oz cup a day, you can save $1126 a year ($94 a month).

A bonus is that you can choose exactly the milk you prefer. Since I only use whole milk for my coffee, I choose non-homogenized organic milk from a small farmer, and occasionally I add real vanilla extract to the bottle, so I get that beautiful aroma in the morning.

If you truly enjoy the ritual and luxury of going to a cafe and drinking your coffee there, I am not trying to take that from you. Some women use their local cafe as their office, and there is a lot to save compared to an office space. However, if you don't enjoy the hassle of getting your coffee and you spend five extra minutes every morning driving to the cafe and then waiting five minutes for your coffee, you could save 56 hours a year (4+ hours a month).

Feel free to use the space below to design your ideal coffee moment - and make it yours. This daily coffee ritual isn't just about taste or money. It is about reclaiming your time, honoring your choices, and defining what luxury means on your terms. In other words, it is you taking steps towards standing in Quiet Power. Choosing slow mornings and joy over convenience is surprisingly radical in a fast-paced world. This moment is for you.

Describe your ideal ritual of *morgenhygge*:

What is your favorite choice of coffee?

What do you need to make it at home?

Where can you buy quality beans - online or in a local roastery?

What is your choice of thermo if you wanna take it to go?

When can you start this new ritual?

List the ways you might save time and money - for example, the cost of your daily café latte compared to what it takes to make it yourself at home:

How much will you save in a year? $_____

How much time will you save in a year? _____ hours

The Belarusian students risked everything for the freedom to gather. What small act of defiance could you practice today to feel more untamed?

What intuitive knowledge lives in you, maybe passed down from women before you, that you haven't fully honored yet?

Feel free to share any extra reflections that come to mind here:

Enjoy!

While you're sipping an aromatic cup of your favorite coffee, let me entertain you with a story from my life in Denmark. Like many women, I had mistaken exhaustion for achievement.

Contrast living

kontraster

Would you believe me if I say that contrast living is the real secret to a life of Quiet Luxury?

In Copenhagen, I was a manager of a health center, which took up many hours of my week. At the end of every workday, I felt that I was constantly behind. Carefree living was very far away.

One rainy afternoon, I put on my rain gear and jumped on my brand-new, white mountain bike. I had just bought it for the prominent raise I negotiated when I accepted the position.

Going fast down the hill, my thoughts still back at work - all of a sudden I was flying. A car had blocked my way when taking a right turn, and it overlooked me. It all happened so fast. My bike crumbled on impact, and I flew over the hood of the car and landed on the wet asphalt, finally gliding to a stop in absolute agony further down the street.

The pain was unbelievable. My knees had hit on impact, and I managed to keep my head up because I was not wearing a helmet. I folded into a fetal position and screamed in pain and shock. Before I knew it, people were around me, putting a folded jacket under my head, repeating comforting words, telling me that I was very lucky, that the ambulance was on its way.

A woman with a kind face laughed a bit and shook her head. "Wow, it looked like you could actually fly", she whispered in disbelief. "Thank goodness you are okay!" I remember rain started falling from the sky. It looked so surreal from my position on the ground.

Shortly after the ambulance arrived and two kind medics checked me over and got me out of the rain. When they were checking my vitals, we could all hear the elderly driver, who cut me off, telling the crowd outside that it was my fault, that I had been driving recklessly.

One of the medics went back outside and told her to give him her name, address, and phone number for insurance purposes. He was very curt with her.

First, she refused, but with so many witnesses around, she eventually relented. Unbelievable, the medic murmured, coming back in. He had my crumpled bike with him. "Let us bring this with us", he smiled.

Even in my shock, I was overwhelmed. So many kind people were going out of their way to help me. His colleague had found my mobile and asked for a phone number for Jan, my boyfriend at the time. He told him to meet us at *Riget*, the main hospital in Copenhagen.

At the emergency room, they confirmed that nothing was broken but that my right kneecap had been shattered. In the name of rehabilitation, a nurse gave me some disinfectant towelettes and taught me how to clean up my wounds and pick gravel out of my palms, while we waited for the x-rays.

Even though I work in rehab too, I was startled that I had to do it myself, but I found out later that it is an efficient way to get people out of shock. Give them a task to focus on.

Jan picked me and my bike up in the early evening. I think he realized how lucky I had been when he saw the state of the bike. We managed to climb the stairs to our apartment on the 5th floor, me hanging off his tall frame, because both my knees were so swollen that I could not bend them. Settling into our bed, I already dreaded calling my boss in the morning.

When Jan woke me up with a steaming hot cortado, the reality was that I could not leave the bed. I barely managed the restroom, even with his help. There is nothing like having your partner help you to the toilet, am I right?

Reaching my boss, she didn't let me finish explaining before insisting that she would send a taxi for me, so I could get to the office. In disbelief, I had to insist that I was stuck at home and that I was lucky not to be at the hospital.

I knew she was desperate because I had taken over a department during a time of turbulence, but still. She finally relented, and I had a few days off. It struck me how easily women's pain can be dismissed. We're expected to keep producing. To keep smiling.

So what does this have to do with living a life in contrast?

I was not aware of the hamster wheel I had created for myself with this demanding job. Every day was a copy of the next. I would look forward to spending time with my friends after work, but gradually, I did not have the energy, and even on the weekends, I mostly stayed at home to catch up on sleep. I stopped living and started surviving.

Like many women, I had mistaken exhaustion for achievement. Waking up in the morning with no energy, dreading the workday ahead of me. I had climbed that career ladder fast, but I realized that I had lost myself in the process. The accident brought back contrasts to my life.

The first big contrast was the relief after the pain subsided. What a relief! Then came the reality that I could not bike, hike, or even dance for months after the accident. My quality of life was reduced significantly. It gave me a pause, though. My life could have ended right there, or I could have lost mobility.

The rehab afterwards was hard, but with the help of a skilled physiotherapist, I gradually got most of my function back in my knees and eventually could go back to biking.

The frequent appointments with the physiotherapist gave me a needed break and a contrast to the stressful work environment. Wanting more breaks like this, I started scheduling a massage after work. It was heaven and connected me to my body again.

That was how I met Inuk, a body-SDS therapist with native roots from Greenland. I traded massage for body-SDS, and I fell in love. The moments we spent together in silence, as he worked the tension from my body, were as healing as the treatment itself.

The contrast between pain and pleasure wove itself into my life, carrying that exquisite sense of feeling like a woman again - alive, desired. The energy between us was intoxicating. It cracked open a space in my stressful life, revealing that there was more to living than work. In that space, an untamed woman awoke.

Living a life with contrast means reclaiming your rhythms, your body, and your energy - in a world that tends to teach women to give too much.

My Latina girlfriends have a gift for creating contrast in their lives. They instinctively understand the importance of play as a counterbalance to work. When I lived in Mexico, I knew that if I called one of them on a whim, she'd be up for a break in the sun, before heading back to work - recharged and smiling.

Whatever you do, do not try to be a one-woman army; include and lean on the people you naturally connect with. I was lucky to choose well when it came to my current partner, Fernando, though it took a few tries to find the right match. You will hear more about that later - as well as my adventures with Inuk.

When I get absorbed in my work, the contrasts in my days tend to blur. That's where Fernando comes in, my personal travel agent in disguise. He bounces ideas off me until we land on yet another adventure. And when we need a bigger reset, we pack our backpacks and disappear for a few days or weeks away from home.

Even small contrasts can create big joy. For instance, go for a walk during your lunch break and breathe in the fresh air as a contrast to sitting at your desk. Let's start with one. What can you do right now to create a contrast?

Then have a close and honest look at your current life. Are you happy and content, or do you long for a stronger connection to your untamed self?

How can you consciously use contrasts to become happier in your unique life?

.

What would that look like daily?

Weekly?

Monthly?

It is a human condition to want things we cannot get, but the grass is not always greener on the other side. A lot of people with an unlimited budget will start to experience fewer contrasts in their lives. When I got the job as a manager, I celebrated with an expensive bottle of champagne, but shortly after that soured in my mouth, so to speak.

When you can always fly business class, the champagne might taste less good. Also, the people you drink your champagne with matter more than you think, and no money in the world can buy friends. So let us challenge this human condition where we quickly take things for granted. Build your everyday life on the principle of contrasts.

Almost everyone I know in Denmark does Winter swimming combined with a sauna afterward. It might sound extreme, and I will be the first to admit that I can barely go in the ocean even in the Danish Summer because it is so cold. But think about this: If you add a bit of discomfort, you will appreciate the contrast.

The equivalent of this is, of course, the famous Wim Hof cold showers. My partner is really into this, so I, too, have started taking hot showers ending in a cold spray. I am challenging myself to see just how cold and how long I can do this.

Cold showers or a plunge into winter water is more than a dare. It is a way to awaken every cell in your body.

For most women, the icy shock stirs circulation, lifts mood, sharpens focus, and even nudges the metabolism awake. It can soften inflammation, strengthen the immune system, and leave you standing taller, more present in your skin. You step out not just warmer, but more alive - proof that meeting the cold with courage can ignite a quiet, lasting fire within.

For me, snorkeling is the height of Quiet Luxury. Slipping beneath the surface and entering that vivid, hidden world of corals and creatures reminds me of the magic of the planet we share. I've met whale sharks, sea turtles, schools of radiant fish, and squid, even the occasional octopus or a drowsy manatee.

And yet, it's the contrast that makes it so exquisite. To arrive there usually means rising early, bargaining with a stranger, taking a boat, and braving the often-chilly water. Later comes the ritual of rinsing away the salt and restoring my hair with a deep mask. Effort and beauty, grit and grace - always, contrasts.

When I returned home after the seminar in Vilnius, my big, comfortable bed felt like heaven, as you can probably imagine. Contrasts are addictive because you get all those natural happy hormones bouncing around in your body.

If this is not your thing, try smaller contrasts. What can you do right now to get yourself off the sofa and add a small contrast to your everyday life?

It can be anything that makes you feel like you have achieved something meaningful through a small discomfort. We are looking to make new habits for a more luxurious lifestyle.

Maybe something really small: I just hand-washed my silk slip since it can't go in the machine. It only took 10 minutes, yet it sat in the basket for weeks because it was not in my routine. Now my nights are more comfortable and luxurious.

How will it make you feel after a small discomfort?

Add any further reflections below:

How about we carve out a little extra time for that exquisite feeling of having all the time in the world - simply by saying no to obligations you never chose yourself.

Say no

sig nej

The ability to say no will set you free.

Women are conditioned to take care of those around them and to put their own needs aside - more so than men. A chilling example is how serial killer Ted Bundy exploited this cultural pattern. You have likely seen one of the many documentaries or listened to the podcasts.

By pretending to have a broken arm in a cast, he would ask young women in broad daylight to help him carry books or load his car. Most women overruled their inner voice telling them something felt wrong, choosing instead to be polite and helpful. That willingness gave him the access he needed to abduct them.

However, at least one young woman trusted her instincts and refused to go with him. Refusing to be tamed, trusting her instincts.

This is, of course, an extreme case, but it proves the point. If you don't already listen to that inner voice of yours - start now.

Daily, it is about choosing who and what you allow into your life. As Viveura so beautifully puts it:

> "The luxury mindset encourages refinement and inspires you to be the curator of your life. It reminds you to be discerning about who and what you allow in your life and to pursue quality over all else."
>
> Viveura

After my bike accident, I still felt obligated to my employees, and soon I lost myself in the hamster wheel again. As a woman, I, too, had been conditioned well by society; I automatically put my own needs second.

An added reason for my deep commitment was that my employees were once my valued colleagues. When I was a health consultant, I was part of a group of about sixteen professionals who were truly dedicated to making a difference. Though our backgrounds were different, we worked as one - a team built on trust, laughter, and shared purpose.

Our manager at the time believed in us. He gave us the freedom to work flexible hours and trusted that we would deliver - and we did, often going above and beyond. But when he left, everything changed. Upper management stepped in, and the culture shifted overnight. Rules replaced trust. The framework that once gave us energy now felt like a cage.

I share this because of what happened next. As a team, we resisted. We said *no* - not with anger, but with integrity. We presented our well-documented results and stood together in quiet solidarity. To this day, I am proud of how we handled it. Our *collective no* was powerful - a reminder that boundaries can unite as much as they protect.

When I later became a manager myself, my goal was to make a difference – perhaps a little naïvely.

In the process, I lost something precious: the camaraderie that once made work feel alive. But every *no* also creates space for something new. For me, that came in the form of Charlotte, a co-manager who became my ally and confidante amid the chaos.

Sometimes we would take our meetings to walk & talks in the forest. Her energy and quiet strength became a steady compass, for me, and for the team. I still carry that with me, along with her love for Danish baked sweets. I can't eat a *rombolle* (a large soft cocoa truffle) without smiling at the thought of her.

In the professional world, it became clear to me how powerful a collective *no* could be but in our private lives, the same principle holds its quiet weight.

Every boundary we set is an act of self-respect. It is how we teach others what matters to us. Yet for many women, saying *no* still feels like a risk, as if love and belonging depend on constant agreement. Learning to say no in the intimate spaces of life is often harder than in the professional ones, but it's also where the deepest transformation begins.

But let me not get lost in the details, let's get back to the story:

Half a year later, I was biking to work again and bam! A car door from a taxi opened right in front of me, and once again I found myself on the cold, hard asphalt. This time, though, I got up right away. My left hand had taken a hit, and my brand-new rain gear was ruined, but I was just relieved that I got away with minor injuries.

I almost laughed in shock and astonishment because this was nearly a repeat of the first accident. Caring and supportive people gathered around me and offered their assistance.

It turned out to be a famous soccer player from the Danish national team, FCK, who was responsible. He did not orient himself before opening the car door, but loudly blamed the taxi driver for not warning him that he had pulled up at a bike lane. For insurance purposes, the witnesses gave me their phone numbers, and so did the taxi driver, because it did not seem like this millionaire sports star would compensate me.

What seems almost like insanity to me now, all I could think about at that point, was that I would be late for a meeting. I jumped on the bike and headed off, driving with one arm, ignoring the pain.

In hindsight, these accidents proved to be a true gift. If you believe in some version of a spiritual force, you will probably agree that the Universe was trying to change my path. Just like in the world of Hans Christian Andersen, something magical happened.

My left hand turned out to be in a bad state, and I soon realized that I had to go to the emergency room after my workday. Before I got that far, I happened to have a meeting with my network of female entrepreneurs. These women-in-business (WIB) were brilliant, independent entrepreneurs in different areas.

Upon arrival, I entertained them with this second bike accident, and they stared at me in disbelief. What are the odds of two bike accidents like this?

The atmosphere at our meetings is always relaxed and focused on how we can help each other. One of the women, Anabella, asked if she should heal my hand, which was now more than double the size and had started throbbing. I joked that it would save me a trip to the hospital, so why not? I did not really believe in it, but I thought it couldn't hurt. During the meeting, she simply held my hand between hers, and it felt nice and warm, maybe a bit tingly.

Finally ending my day, I had no energy to sit in line at the emergency room, so I decided to go in the early morning instead. I woke up tired and sore all over and headed straight for the espresso machine. Then, remembering the healing, I looked at my hand - it looked almost normal. Only a small scar on the inner side of my thumb was new. I was astonished. How could this be?

This was the beginning of the end of my career as a manager. I realized that life is too short to give your precious time to a work environment that was becoming more and more inhumane. I finally found my voice again, and it was a *hell no*.

I knew I wanted a change in my life. Ever since I spent a year in Australia when I was a teenager, I have wanted to try my chances outside of Denmark.

In Danish, we have a word, *udlængsel*, that has no true counterpart in English. It describes a deep, quiet longing to explore the world. Not just from dissatisfaction, but from a sense that something within us is still unmet. As a restless teenager, I recognized this feeling in the poetry of Thomas Boberg, which became a great source of inspiration.

There is a part of me that resists being fully tamed, perhaps a trace of my Viking past, when boldness and movement were part of our nature. *Udlængsel* is the soul's whisper toward the wild - toward expansion, aliveness, and something we have almost forgotten.

Longing for the unknown, I began searching for work in humanitarian organizations and, at the same time, ended my relationship with Jan. We had grown apart - I was no longer the same person. It was time to put my own needs first and seek adventure.

That spring, for the first time in my life, I asked a man out. Inuk turned me down at first because of the client–therapist boundary. I moved my massage appointments elsewhere, and he agreed to meet for coffee.

That first date felt like two kids discovering a new world together. Every time I looked into his eyes, I felt a strong connection to him. We would spend time together exploring Copenhagen with curiosity, and he helped expand my world.

Another unexpected gift from that stressful work environment was Jacob, my brilliant therapist. At least I had had the sense to ask for a supervisor when I accepted the challenging manager role. He became my saving grace, with his sharp wit and holistic way of seeing the world.

With a hint of humor, he commented on my timing - falling in love with a man in the midst of chaos. Inuk became my escape, a doorway into a world of magic and freedom.

Strangely, we never conventionally had sex, but we explored an almost innocent connection on every level - both of us savoring our newfound freedom after years in relationships that had burned out. Together, we leaned into the strong energy between us, experimenting with tantra. Today, we share a precious friendship, built on the courage to speak openly and deeply.

At the end of Summer, my sister Ann invited me to a reunion party in Berlin with her friends. She is only two years younger than I, so we grew up as pseudo-twins.

Life had pulled us in different directions, and she had left Germany years ago and now lives outside of London. I admire her deeply for the ability to build a career and settle in a new country so fully, without looking back. However, it also means that we do not see each other as often as we would like.

Returning to Berlin was an opportunity to come full circle for both of us.

In the 00s, Ann went to Germany as part of her uni studies. If you want to know the true essence of women's capability to stand in their Quiet Power, have a look at the psychological patterns in the KZ camps during the Second World War. That's what she did.

Not surprisingly, many women formed strong support networks - sharing food, offering emotional care, and protecting each other when possible. These small acts of solidarity often helped them survive longer than men.

When my sister wasn't studying, however, she enjoyed the nightlife. I would visit her and knew most of her friends from back then. And just like ten years earlier, I was high on life, enjoying my colorful single life. Free and untamed once again. We went clubbing like we used to. It was a blast!

On the second night, something unexpected happened - I found myself kissing her former roommate, Fernando. It felt like pure ecstasy.

The trans woman DJing at the nightclub *Treasure* turned it into an almost otherworldly experience. Her untamed tunes enveloped us. She reminded me that being untamed is about belonging, fully, in your own skin. I could only imagine the journey it took for her to arrive there - not born a woman, yet fully claiming womanhood.

From that moment, everything seemed to fall into place. When I returned to Copenhagen after the weekend, I knew I had to see him again. Three weeks later, I showed up at his door with shaky hands and a bottle of gin from the airport. The connection was immediate, I fell deeply and passionately in love with him.

Sometimes life comes at you fast. After a year spent together, divided between Berlin and Copenhagen, we leaped into the unknown. He, too, was ready to leave his life in Berlin.

I had a bit of savings, so we set off to travel through Europe and Africa for three months, exploring potential spots to start a microbrewery. The plan was simple: Fernando, who had studied brewing, would make the beer, and I would run the rest.

That journey eventually led us to Mexico because we found out that Europe couldn't provide the strong network we needed, but Tijuana could. Just across the border from San Diego, Fernando's hometown had a thriving craft beer culture.

When I finally took the big step of leaving Denmark to begin a new life in Mexico, I, all of a sudden, had very little money but all the time in the world. I started laughing again. I realized that I had stopped laughing carefree because of the stress of my everyday life. Not surprisingly, I also slept through the night again.

Nothing pulls you into the present quite like a big crisis. Once again, I was reminded that joy lives in contrast. For years, I savored Mexico - the freedom of a country with fewer rules, among people who cherish life's small pleasures, like a good meal and an ice-cold margarita in the sun. I need that Latin spirit more than ever now that we no longer live there.

Saying no to our life in Mexico was not easy, but that *no* opened the door to new expressions of Quiet Power and Luxury.

Is there anything in your life today that you want to say no to?

Can you carve out more time daily by saying no to something you have no real interest in?

Do you allow the right people into your life, or is it time to be more selective?

When and with whom do you laugh? Can you get more of that in your everyday life?

If more thoughts arise, you can note them here:

This is an area where you can save an abundance of time.

Imagine that every time you say no to something, it gives you the time and energy to do something more interesting. For instance, you decide to spend your birthday at a spa hotel with your best girlfriend instead of inviting the entire family over for coffee and cake. You might avoid losing energy navigating family drama and instead recharge in Quiet Luxury.

Consider how many hours and how much energy you can potentially reclaim:

Estimated hours saved in a year: _____

Estimated money saved in a year: $ _____

The ChatGPT assistant suggests a journaling sheet with a rating: Energy-Giving | Energy-Neutral | Energy-Draining. It can remind you to honor energy-giving choices.

If you need help actually saying no, it can draft kind but firm text or email templates to decline (family) obligations or step back from overwork. It can also help you calculate exactly how much you can save, of course.

While you carve out a clearer path in your life, let us have a look at the concept of *hygge* and how to make it a cozy escape from the world outside your doors.

Scandinavian
coziness

hygge

Hygge is an efficient and pleasurable way of creating more contrasts in your life. A way to gather energy for your adventures.

When I visit Denmark, I make sure to go in Spring or Summer when the sun is high in the sky. I catch up with my friends and family, staying at their respective homes. One of the best places to deal with jetlag is in my friend Tina's summerhouse north of Copenhagen. It is in the forest close to the beach, so we go for long walks, catching up. Taking in the fresh smells and all the green - a beautiful contrast to the calm, desert I live in in New Mexico.

Tina always brews a pot of tea, and we settle in, inside or out, depending on the mood and the light. We skip the small talk and sink straight into the deeper layers of life.

Earlier this year, she published a book about exactly that; *Fortæl mig din historie* (Tell Me Your Story) – an invitation to more meaningful conversations. The tea itself could just as well be plain hot water; it is secondary to the moment. At home, I sometimes make a cup for myself, but it's never quite the same.

Later, I need the vibrant life of Copenhagen and will stay with my friend Mie. We catch up late into the night after her little girl has been tucked in. We put on facial masks and laugh and drink Cremant. Sometimes one of us will exclaim; "ej er det her ikke bare hyggeligt!" (Oh, isn't this just a feel-good moment!). Even when her baby was tiny, she still made space for me in her home.

When I have had a good, strong dose of friends and Copenhagen, I head to the countryside where my family lives. Getting spoiled by my mom with homemade food and cake straight out of the oven is priceless.

My mom is nearly deaf, so instead of talking nonstop, we often watch a movie together or enjoy her garden. One of our traditions is also to drive to the beach to walk and pick up shells or go to a Thrift store to browse retro mugs or crystal glasses.

Last year, we had a death in the family, so I went in November, and the weather was just as dark and wet as I remembered. We simply pretended that it was Xmas already and did all the traditional things. Food, hot drinks, decorations, and Xmas movies.

I admire the way she enjoys her own company and the small things in life instead of focusing on the limits. Music is a big part of my life, and I often think of what it must be like to live a life without that luxury.

These are all examples of Danish *hygge* moments.

So what exactly is *hygge*?

Like I mentioned in the intro, *hygge* can be defined as "conscious coziness". In short, a carefree moment you consciously aim to carve out of your busy day - either alone or with loved ones. Often with elements that stimulate your senses. You can also define it as a Quiet Luxury moment in your everyday life.

Hygge is that moment during the day when you feel at ease. It is when your senses are focused on the joy of your morning coffee, waking up to a new day of possibilities. Or when a pot of simmering chili is giving off mouth-watering aromas, resulting in a meal where everyone gathers around the table.

Or it is that moment when you cozy up with a blanket in your favorite *hygge-hjørne* with a good book and perhaps the dog at your feet. A *hyggehjørne* is a dedicated spot in your home where you feel safe and relaxed, for instance, a favorite armchair. If you are a typical woman, your life is filled with chores and activities, so you need this moment to balance out the day. It is where you gain energy by connecting to your body.

When *hygge* became a popular concept in the US a few years ago, it was great to see piles of blankets in the cafes with a sign that said *hygge*. Out of curiosity, I read some books from my fellow Danes and was a bit surprised at how much they could squeeze out of a concept that for me was simply a feeling of everyday contentment.

Like anyone else, I am, of course, a product of my culture, so I hadn't given it a thought that *hygge* could inspire other cultures, especially because it is strongly connected to the cold and dark weather in Denmark.

When I use it in this context, it is because I recognize the value of these moments. I notice that *hygge* sometimes gets glamorized too much - an easy mistake when you are proud of your culture, but not what I consider it to be. I would like to point out that it is a down-to-earth feeling of comfort, and therefore, for everyone, not super hipster like it sometimes is made out to be.

Scandinavians are messy and overindulge, too. We eat too many sweets and spend way too much time binge-watching TV. We are not any better than others. If anything, Scandinavians are often very serious and could learn from other cultures to laugh and be a bit more spontaneous.

Latin America seems to embrace the now with a presence that I deeply admire. Salsa, cumbia, and similar dances are such a joy. It would suit Scandinavians to get out of their minds and into their bodies, but I guess we have *Dogme 95* instead as a testament to our darker Scandinavian culture.

The movement began in Copenhagen in 1995, when two Danish filmmakers, Lars von Trier and Thomas Vinterberg, felt that cinema had become too artificial, too dominated by expensive effects and shallow emotions. So they wrote a radical manifesto, a set of rules called "The Vow of Chastity."

The movement demanded artistic purity. Filmmakers who joined agreed to use handheld cameras, natural light, and real sound - to film on location and, perhaps most radically, to give up personal credit. Each film was created in the spirit of collaboration, stripping away illusion until only the raw human story remained.

Hygge can soothe, but it can also sedate. When comfort turns into a way of numbing, we risk losing touch with what's real. That is perhaps why Danish filmmakers so often go the other way – straight into discomfort.

They expose the fragile beauty of what we try to hide - our fears, desires, and contradictions. It's the opposite of *hygge*, and yet it serves the same purpose: to make us feel alive. Where *hygge* softens the edges of life, *Dogme* reminds us not to fall asleep in them.

My examples of *hygge* moments:

- A long walk in the cold, then coming home to the warm smell of simmering food my partner is cooking

- Cozy up on the sofa with a book from a favorite author and a blanket

- Grilling in the garden and watching the dogs and cats play

- Staying over at a friend's house, chatting while putting on facemasks

- Reading fairy tales for my nephew and niece before bedtime is true *hygge*

- Having a marathon retro movie night with sweets and popcorn

- Listening to Xmas hits while baking with friends or family

Prioritize some moments of *hygge* every day. If you have a bad day, try to use it as something to look forward to. Consider that the whole day isn't ruined because it might get better after a mental getaway with your favorite book or a walk with the dog. This way, you can find your way back to Quiet Power and Luxury.

How can you carve out a bit of quality time on your own?

What would your preferred *hygge* moment be - alone or with others?

What would your *hygge* moments look like? List them here:

-
-
-
-
-
-
-

Do you have the necessities for creating *hygge*? Perhaps a blanket, armchair, book, woolen socks, candlelight, or clutter-free surroundings?

Hygge balances seriousness with play. What playful or even silly ritual could you add to your life that would soften the edges of responsibility?

Where can you save time for these blissful moments of *hygge*?

I pay $14.95 a month for my book subscription. I read at least 3 books a week, plus listen to commercial-free podcasts. So if an average book costs around $10, I save $1296 a year on books alone.

Many libraries offer free apps - you can consider asking your ChatGPT to check your area for this option and save even more money.

How much can you save on book or podcast subscriptions yearly? $ _____

Recently, it was Black Friday, and we considered getting an iPad or a Kindle that we could share, but we ended up deciding against it.

Realistically, I use my MacBook or my mobile for everything, and after some good thinking, we realized that we do not need it. I simply read books on my mobile phone, and it works.

Consider asking your ChatGPT assistant other ways to save money. When I did this, it suggests that you can save money by making homemade or experience-based gifts as more meaningful options: "Instead of buying birthday gifts, offer someone a home-cooked meal, a walk-and-talk in nature, or a movie night with cozy snacks. Connection is the ultimate luxury."

Prompt suggestions:

How many gifts can you replace with cozy shared experiences this year?
Will you estimate my yearly savings?

If more thoughts arise, you can note them here:

Now, let us elevate your *hygge* moments with some luxurious bubbles.

Bubbles

bobler

I associate fizzy drinks with having a good time with my friends. How about you?

With help from Fernando's family and friends, we managed to open Bajer Brewing, a brewery and taproom, within a couple of years in Tijuana.

Our vision was to take some of our beloved Berlin vibes with us, including the electronic music scene. We worked around the clock and had so much fun doing it. Our world evolved around fizzy drinks.

Not only craft beer, but I also made semi-dry sparkly meads in the Viking tradition of Denmark. It started as a fun experiment, but soon, half of our taps were serving fruity meads. I enjoyed making something hands-on while handling a thousand other things that come with running a small company.

As a woman navigating a male-dominated brewing scene, I found joy in crafting my path - blending tradition, innovation, and you could say, a bit of rebellion in every fizzy pour.

I met some strong, capable women in my first years. They helped me navigate Mexican culture and gave me the gift of sisterhood.

My *cuñada* Abril helped me navigate this new world, and we bonded over creative projects. She took me to her sister-in-law Perla's hair salon. Perla turned out to be a savvy hairdresser, entrepreneur, and a much-needed soundboard on how to be a female boss in Mexico.

It turned out that Perla adored the Danish series *Rita*. She said it felt oddly familiar – this loud, unapologetic woman who loved fiercely, made mistakes, and refused to fit neatly into anyone's expectations.

There seems to be something in the Mexican soul that resonates with that kind of honesty, a shared appetite for emotion, for being fully alive.

Maybe that's what connects our cultures: beneath the surface differences, both celebrate the messiness of being human. Whether through Rita's irreverence or the Dogme filmmakers' brutal honesty, we keep finding our way back to the same truth – that aliveness is worth more than perfection.

At a cannabis festival, I met Armenui, a proud *tijuanense* singer and creative. I was serving mead and beer to promote our brewery, and we started talking. The next day, she came to the taproom where we made plans for a collab on CBD-infused drinks and live music.

That was the beginning of a precious, passionate friendship.

We would hang out at her music studio. Sometimes share a bottle of local bubbles and a line while listening to music, or she would sing for me. A creative space where other artists would drop by and share stories. Armenui's openness - to love, to beauty, to both men and women - feels like a natural extension of her spirit.

If anything, women are excellent networkers. We will get back to this in a later chapter.

Armenui and her girlfriends taught me how to deal with the police if I were approached while being on my own. These women were not to be tamed; they would carry hidden weapons just in case. Despite Tijuana's reputation, I felt safe walking the streets, even at night. I would often walk the short walk home from our bar alone.

I refuse to make my world smaller because of fear. Fear is what is stopping women from standing in their Quiet Power, from pursuing a life in freedom.

I have traveled the world, often solo, and most of the places that have a reputation for high crimes are just that. A reputation. An option is to take a self-defense class. It might not only expand your sense of freedom, but it could be a powerful (and fun) experience to share with a girlfriend.

Later, craft cocktails on tap followed. I would make 11 gallons (40 liters) of Mezcal Mule or G&T. Always made with natural ingredients like organic ginger root and herbs. This way, we did not compromise on quality and could still keep the price down.

We had a very clear goal to create a space where everyone was welcome. You might not know this, but Tijuana has a very inclusive culture and a vibrant LGBTQ+ community. Over time, the brewery became a speakeasy scene evolving around local DJs. Fernando and his brother Franco are both talented, experienced DJs, so it was a natural element to add to the bar. In that space, I could dance and connect with my kind of people. Good times!

Now that we live in Albuquerque, I rekindle the luxury of craft cocktails by making smaller amounts for friends. Like many women before me, I have learned how to turn fermenting and flavoring into expressions of freedom and creativity.

I use Drinkmate because it can also carbonate other non-pulp drinks. In essence, you can fizz up the Prosecco, mead, or beer that went flat in the fridge or make your homemade non-alcoholic cider from your cold-pressed apple juice. Whatever you can imagine. It is cordless, so you can place it anywhere in your kitchen.

If you, too, have a habit of drinking fizzy drinks or sparkling water, you can consider buying a soda maker. The savings are big if you like to hydrate with flavored soda or cans of seltzer. You can save at least $45 a month (or $540 a year) if you drink two cans a day. It will also save you the trouble of going to the store and taking up space in the refrigerator. Isn't cooking so much easier when you can see what ingredients you have in the fridge?

Together, Fernando and I drink more than 3 liters a day, so we always have two bottles in the fridge. I calculated that we save more than $1800 a year this way. I also have a weakness for ginger beer, but most brands are too sweet for my taste, so I make a concentrate of fermented ginger root that is available to fizz up whenever I feel like it. This also comes in handy when I am in the mood for a boozy Mezcal Mule.

You can make any flavor you like, either with homemade syrups or by buying ready-made syrups. Maybe you wanna use the maple syrup with real vanilla that you made for your coffee as an alternative to another sweet soda? If you prefer unsweetened bubbles, slices of cucumber or citrus, or herbs like rosemary or mint will turn hydrating into a Quiet Luxury experience.

As with coffee, you can bring it to go, of course. Just make sure that your bottle can handle the pressure of the CO_2 and keep it cold. I like the minimalist Danish brand by Lars Nysøm. The stylish design adds a bit of glamour to my hikes.

Transporting water and other drinks does make a huge CO_2 imprint on the planet - it is heavy stuff. On that note, it would be amazing if we could stop restaurants from importing expensive, fancy sparkling water. Be part of a movement and ask if they carry local brands.

A typical can of Coke contains about 10 teaspoons of refined sugar (39 grams). If you're looking to cut down on sugar, try carbonating water and adding a splash of tart cherry juice or a squeeze of fresh grapefruit with a sprig of rosemary. Or bring Mexico into your home with a spicy tamarind soda.

These simple swaps can help you ease into less sweet, more natural alternatives while still feeling indulgent. By making your simple syrup, you can avoid corn syrup and add some micronutrients. It can be an easy way to get used to drinking less sweet versions.

Give it that luxury feeling by choosing a beautiful, heavy crystal glass with ice cubes and maybe a slice of lime. Or occasionally a splash of quality rum or tequila.

When have you felt most untamed while raising a glass - not because of what you drank, but because of who you were with and how free you felt?

What is your favorite fizzy drink?

How many cans or bottles of fizzy drinks do you drink a day?

If it is a soda with sugar or artificial ingredients, what can you replace it with?

What is your choice of a thermo bottle if you wanna take it to go?

How much do you save a year if you change to a soda maker? $ _____

If your fridge has a built-in ice maker, you can save money and hassle here as well. If you, for instance, use a medium-sized (16 lb) bag in a fortnight, it will save you $72 a year.

Note your potential time and money savings here - for instance, switching sugary cans of soda to a soda maker:

How much money can you save yearly if you add it all together? $ _____

How much time can you save yearly? _____ hours

If more reflections come to mind, write them here:

While you sit with your bubbles in your *hyggehjørne*, let's reimagine your home - not just as a place to live, but as the haven you' have always longed for.

Home

hjem

When you enter your home, how do you feel? Are you pleased and relaxed? Annoyed or stressed out? Is your home clutter-free, or have other members of your household made a mess? Is the kitchen how you left it in the morning?

How many women do you know who often end up cleaning up after other members of their family? I imagine too many!

For a lot of women, this is a significant stressor in their lives and one that makes them argue with their partners almost daily. If you are single, please enjoy the fact that any mess is all yours. If not, it is most definitely worth an effort to make sure your family will clean up after themselves and share the daily chores.

The reward is instant. You will feel that you got a new designer home and more carefree time for *hygge*. If you design your house so that everything has a dedicated place, everyone in the family knows where to put things. The fewer things you have, the less clutter and thereby a calmer atmosphere in your home.

Minimalism does not mean living in a clinically clean home or that you need to throw away your favorite books, but it aims for a stress-free environment. When you choose every item with care, you will appreciate it more. For instance, do not buy a cheap shoe rack, but consider putting up hooks on the wall so the clutter gets away from the floor, and it is much easier to clean up.

For an instant improvement in your mood, begin with the lowest-hanging fruit. You know those things that bother you every single day but turn out to take a very short time to fix.

If every time you open your fridge, you cannot find anything, organizing and running a cloth over the surface will probably take you around 5 minutes. If you share with your family, negotiate where different items belong, and maybe buy fewer groceries at a time, or consider buying a fridge that better suits your needs.

Put a beautiful handmade basket near the door where everyone can easily throw in their beanies, gloves, scarves, and so on instead of cluttering up the entrance. If possible, buy it from women in emerging economies like India or Africa. The key is to give every little thing in your house a home, while supporting other women.

A rule of thumb is also to buy quality. Imagine that you will keep this item forever instead of falling into the consumer trap of cheaper items that you have to replace.

In Mexico, there's a common saying: *"Lo que es barato es caro"*. What's cheap often turns out to be expensive. Meaning that if you go for a cheaper option, you will most likely end up paying more in the end. What you want to do instead is hit that sweet spot of value for money.

If you tend to buy small, cheap items that you happen to find while out shopping, consider whether those items suit your home or if they end up as clutter. You can save time and money by replacing this habit with a focus on each room and investing in fewer, higher-quality items that truly fit.

The same way that you end up with a wardrobe, you wear instead of buying spur-of-the-moment items that end up in the back of your closet. Organizing your closets with fewer clothes of higher quality will solve that problem in the same way that your home will be a joy to be in.

How can your ChatGPT assistant support you here? New habits take a lot of energy, so maybe it can take over some of the practical stuff?

In February of 2020, we managed to move into our LOFT apartment in downtown Tijuana just before everything closed down because of COVID-19.

It was exhilarating moving into a brand new home that we could make completely ours, after having rented an apartment for years and before that living with my Mexican mother-in-law.

It had been an intense two months of non-stop working on getting our new home just right. I was an accomplished amateur, having done the interior design for our brewery and taproom already. I now designed a home in an old warehouse with a small local team of four very handy and capable locals, and of course, with input from my partner.

It was really hard work, especially since my Spanish skills were limited, so communication took a lot of energy. But in the end, it was so rewarding.

Our friends and family thought we were nuts, though. The industrial building had been empty for more than five years, and homeless people had broken in and lived in it. For us, however, it was a white canvas and only our imagination was the limit. 2260 square feet (210 m2) of possibilities.

Waking up in our new home was like a dream. Now with time on my hands, I became curious about the theory behind getting the right atmosphere. After a bit of research, when the internet was finally up and running, I found a globally accredited certification in interior design from The Interior Design Institute in Sydney, Australia.

The certification was scheduled to take a year and sounded like the perfect balance of theory and practical modules that I could use directly in our new home. Since the Australian dollar was weak, I got the course for a very good price, so it wouldn't make a big dent in our savings. I was excited and ready to go.

In the end, it took a bit more than a year - they make their students work for it. Gradually, our home took shape with those details only interior design can provide. There is something magical about being in that creative zone and letting ideas meet reality.

We kept the steel curtains covering the front of the building, so we could park the car directly in our home, and it offered privacy and security. We could use luxurious materials inside and simply make it look like a normal warehouse from the outside. Quiet Luxury, right? We did not need to show off and attract intruders.

I wanted to play around with the industrial style that would fit the concrete walls and high ceilings. I located a scrap yard and found old metal doors, cabinets, and even birdcages that I turned into sliding doors, a shower divider, lamps, and a wash cabinet. Recycling and upcycling.

In contrast, I bought designer toilets, luxurious massage shower heads, fossettes, etc., for a more contemporary look.

A very simple principle in interior design is the law of harmony.

Interior design is inspired by the balance of nature because it pleases the senses. So you wanna aim for the colors of your home to be roughly 60% of a calming natural color like white, cream, or gray. It is most likely your walls, floors, and ceiling, as well as your main furniture. To this palette, you add 30% of a similar color in nuances, darker or lighter. The last 10% is your accent color, and here you can go as crazy as you want.

When I chose the color schedule for our home, I chose gold as the accent and even brushed up an original mural on our wall with gold and black. Using a color wheel, it was the perfect contrast to the 60% gray concrete and 30% creamy white walls and furniture.

All the smaller touches, like pillows, lamps, a favorite painting, or maybe even your electric kettle, can have a touch of your accent color. You can also make a designer armchair stand out that way. Think of your accent items as the accessories - just like your wardrobe, they give it that last touch.

We had a budget of $50.000 for everything, including solar energy! I had to be creative. We simply built the entire kitchen in concrete - I used chalk to draw the kitchen on the floor before deciding on the design. It was so much fun. At this time, the Mexican team thought I had lost it. All they saw was garbage I had dragged home from the scrap yard instead of choosing a traditional Mexican style.

The alley behind the building was turned into a long, slim garden area. A large hole in the wall became a breakfast bar in the kitchen, where you could sit and have your morning coffee or share a mezcal with good friends.

To make the hole, the foreman gave me a huge sledgehammer with a grin. During the project, I would eat tacos with the crew for lunch, and we had all become a tight-knit team. He found it amusing that I was so hands-on with the project. A cultural clash, but we made it work.

We hired a company to put solar on the flat roof, and the rest of it was used as a rooftop terrace. If you want to see more pics of the project, feel free to visit @detsign on Instagram.

I like feeling grounded when I sleep, so our quality king-size mattresses were simply put on the floor and covered with high-tread linen and pillows for a minimal look. I recommend organic linen or cotton for the softest feeling, and it lasts a lifetime.

We wanted a playful element in our home, so I even started drawing on the walls, and we put a swing in the living room facing the kitchen. Every time we had guests, it was a joy to see them swing with a big, childish smile on their faces.

The light design is the hardest to get right, and when we moved three years later on new adventures, I honestly still had not gotten it right. However, our current tenant seems to like the darker, cave-like atmosphere. Use this rule of thumb: For a hyggelig atmosphere, go for warm light in little islands around your house. Only direct, sharper light in the kitchen where you work.

So, how is this relevant to you?

This project is an example to give you a few *guldkorn* (gold nuggets) from my certification, so you can give your home the right atmosphere if you haven't already. Whatever style you have, you might wanna consider this:

Is there anything in your home that annoys you and you would like to change/optimize?

Make a project in Todoist of possible changes and change it gradually if you need to save up or go looking for just the right item. Consider if you have some items that you are especially fond of, and include them in your design.

We spend so much time in our homes that optimizing will be worth it. Be mindful that your inner world is reflected in your outer world. We are not aiming for perfectionism here. A home needs to be lived in and a place where you can relax. So whatever that looks like to you, make it yours!

Unfortunately, many modern things you can buy for your home are of poor quality.

If, for instance, your kitchen could do with an upgrade, make sure that you do not end up with cheap plywood cabinets and vinyl tiles on your floor. In a very short time, they will start showing signs of wear and tear because the kitchen is one of the highways of the house. Just think about this: how many times a day do you open and close cabinets to get what you need for snacking, eating, drinking, and cooking?

If you are lucky enough to have a home from the mid-century, consider using some of the original features in your new design. Things from back then were built to last. If you need inspiration, there is unlimited inspiration to find on Pinterest, and your ChatGPT will be happy to help your ideas come to life.

Contrasts in texture are sometimes overlooked. When playing around with smooth, rough, shiny, and matte textures, it adds depth to your design. For instance, throw pillows in different shapes, patterns, and fabrics will make your home more interesting.

Thrift Stores, Facebook market, or antique shops can be a goldmine to find those original items to mix in with more contemporary things. For instance, an original chandelier from an old church could be a valued accent item.

One last point: consider learning to use a basic drill machine so you are not dependent on any man. It is super easy to use when you try it a couple of times, and then you can easily put up a painting on the wall or hooks for whatever. They even come in pink if that's your thing.

There are big savings to be made here.

Furniture is expensive. Interior designers are expensive. If you can find items in Thrift stores that last forever, you are ahead of the game. Mother Earth will thank you for your choices. But most of all, making sure your family knows where everything belongs, you have saved yourself hours of frustration. Be patient and prepare to compromise. Focus on one room at a time.

Now, have a look around your home:

What colors does it have?

Have you purposefully chosen these colors?

Are you happy with the color scheme?

Does it live up to the 60/30/10 rule, somewhat?

Can you do something to get closer to this rule of thumb to create harmony?

Is the furniture placed so that it serves your needs?

Do you already have a *hyggehjørne* or would you like to make one?

Does every item in your home have a designated place, a home?

Does your family know this and take part in putting things away? If not, can you make a plan with them?

Do you (and your family) think that the layout is functional?

Does it give everyone privacy as well as social areas?

If you ask your partner or children, what would they like to add to the new design?

What can you change today?

If you do not have to compromise on anything, what would be different in your home?

Make a list. Do you have anything in the garage or the attic that could become part of your home?

-

-

-

-

-

-

Or that you can sell off or give away if you no longer want it?

Potential changes for the kitchen:

The living room:

The master bedroom:

The bathroom(s):

Any other room(s):

The balcony, terrace or garden:

What boundary could you strengthen in your home so you feel more at peace?

If you stop impulse buying cheap items for $50 a month, you can save $600 a year as well as time. If you sell all the things you no longer use or that do not fit your style anymore, there is most likely money there to spend on quality furniture.

Most of all, there is time to save. If you spend 30 minutes every day cleaning up your home and instead leave these chores to others, you can save 3.5 hours a week (168 hours a year). That is true luxury gained by standing in your Quiet Power.

Note your potential time and money savings here:

How much money can you save in a year? $ _____

How much time can you save in a year? _____ hours

Your ChatGPT can turn into a full-on Interior Designer here if you want it. It can generate digital mood boards using preferred colors, textures, and themes. Visualize design ideas through AI-generated room mockups tailored to your style. Offer a 3D room layout suggestion using the dimensions you provide. Even teach you how to use a power drill.

If you have been using ChatGPT for a while, you can try this prompt: "Tell me what I really need in my home based on everything you know about me". This can help you break away from a traditional home to one that supports your true needs.

Have fun!

Nordic walking

gåtur

"Above all, do not lose your desire to walk. Every day, I walk myself into a state of well-being & walk away from every illness. I have walked myself into my best thoughts, and I know of no thought so burdensome that one cannot walk away from it. But by sitting still, & the more one sits still, the closer one comes to feeling ill. Thus, if one just keeps on walking, everything will be alright."

Søren Kierkegaard

The famous quote here is from the Danish philosopher Søren Kierkegaard, and even though it is from 1847, it is still relevant today.

It makes me think that the benefits of walking are connected to when we were nomads. Something has changed, though. If anything, time is a luxury in our fast-paced society, and it is a moment where you can just be in the now and take in the light and the surroundings. No expectations.

Forget about *hygge* and minimalism - if anything is a testament to Scandinavian culture, it is walking. Hell, we even have a special kind of walk called Nordic Walking. When I lived in Budapest, everyone would tease us Danes that Nordic Walking was off-limits because no one else could keep up with our long strides.

I lived with Trine for four months in Budapest. She is a gentle woman with a fierce, steady heart. When her French husband left her, barely unpacked in their new life, she was suddenly stranded in a foreign country after years of following him around the world.

She had set aside her own hard-earned university degree and career to support his. And yet, when he cheated and the marriage ended, he wasn't legally required to share his income with her. Ten years together, but because the marriage itself was short, French law protected him, not her.

The injustice still stings when I think of it. I've shared her story with many women because it mirrors a quiet pattern that repeats across cultures: brilliant women dimming their power, trusting a man to hold the structure, and discovering too late that the system doesn't hold them in return.

But Trine rose. She chose to stay in Budapest, to rebuild, to nourish her friendships, and eventually she fell in love with a Hungarian man who saw her clearly. Meanwhile, her ex didn't stay long with the young tennis teacher. He lost an extraordinary woman.

Her story is one of reclamation – a reminder that when a woman returns to herself, she becomes untouchable in the best way.

Walking is something everyone can do. Put on your favorite sneakers and leave your house. You might have a thousand excuses for staying in your cozy home, but I promise you that it will be worth it and even addictive over time.

I get a needed break and gather energy when I walk. Every day, the mountains in the background look different. I am so amazed by nature in North America, no matter where I put on my shoes and go for a walk. I wonder why we don't talk more about the unique nature and strong native cultures in the Americas.

Compared to Europe, there is so much space to explore.

If you go about your day feeling guilty or frustrated for missing the gym again, consider simply stepping out of your front door for a short walk. It can be a stroll or a higher-paced Nordic Walking, where you activate your glutes if you take longer strides. You can add hand- or wrist weights if you want a fuller body workout.

Especially for us women, the pressure to 'do it all' can make skipping a workout feel like failure - but walking offers a kinder, more sustainable rhythm.

I wonder if Søren would be surprised if we told him today that studies agree on "walking into a state of well-being"?

For instance, studies from Harvard reveal that walking efficiently boosts your immune function and adds protection during cold and flu season. A study of over 1,000 men and women found that those who walked at least 20 minutes a day, five days a week, had 43% fewer sick days than those who exercised once a week or less. And if they did get sick, it was for a shorter duration, and their symptoms were milder.

Add to that a lower risk of breast cancer, and for instance, walking 6 miles a week can prevent arthritis.

The reward for walking is immediate. Your blood sugar stabilizes, and if you get into a routine, you will gradually lose weight by keeping your muscle mass up and regulating the system. You can even use walking as a distraction when a craving takes over because you are bored or unhappy. This way, you release happy hormones like endorphins, dopamine, and serotonin. When you return, you have most likely forgotten about your craving and come back energized.

If you want to add further rewards, feel free to bring one of your to-go drink options - hot or cold, depending on the weather and time of day. In Denmark, we will almost always end a walk & talk in a nearby cafe as a reward.

In my neighborhood in Albuquerque, I almost always pass two women chatting away in their native tongue as part of their routine. There is something quietly powerful about women walking together, sharing space and stories. It's not just exercise - it's community, connection, and reclaiming time for ourselves.

When I visit Copenhagen, I love meeting up with friends in their neighborhood for a nice long walk to catch up and then go for lunch or a snack somewhere. My friends are busy people, so this works well for everyone. This way I can enjoy all those Danish delicatessen with a good conscience. Fresh air and socializing give you that distinct feeling of *hygge*.

During my last visit in the Spring, I was enjoying the smell of the ocean and the sun on my face while waiting for my friend Mie.

It happened to be close to the statue of the Little Mermaid. I was curiously watching a bus of Japanese tourists excitedly stepping off and heading for the statue that quickly disappeared from view. If you haven't been to Copenhagen, you might not know that the statue of Hans Christian Andersen's famous Mermaid is very small. Placed on the water about 10 feet (3 meters) out, she becomes invisible when tourists crowd around her.

It is a beautiful scene with the Queen's castle in the background and the surrounding gardens, while the guards watching over the castle look like human-sized nutcrackers.

When I saw a bike heading straight at me, I realized that my friend had arrived. Swooshing in for a big hug by simply stopping the bike right in front of me. It earned us some curious glances from the tourists.

Mie parked her bike on the spot, and we headed for the trails away from the touristed area. Often, we have to catch up for a whole year.

She is one of the strongest women I know. When time moved on in her life, and she hadn't met the right man to start a family with, she chose to do it alone. As you can imagine, walking that path solo takes incredible strength.

First, the fertility process itself is brutal. Then came the challenge of reshaping her life around a small child, while still pursuing her career. She has surrounded herself by other remarkable women who support her - and honestly, had she settled for the wrong man, she might have faced even harder struggles.

In deep conversation with pebbles crunching under our feet, we walked around *Kastellet* when suddenly my friend said, "Oh, I guess Queen Mary is out walking her dogs".

With a brief and lightly accented "hi," Mary walked briskly by us with her two beautiful blue-eyed huskies. Her coat was open, and her long, dark hair was blowing in the breeze. Just her and her dogs enjoying some quiet quality time.

Not only do I love that Copenhagen is made for walking and biking, but our celebrities feel comfortable living their normal life like everyone else, without feeling the need to have security with them.

It just happened that we saw her husband, King Frederik, and their two youngest kids biking near *Nyhavn* a couple of days later.

The weather could be the reason why we take long strides and walk quickly in Denmark. If you walk consciously, picking up the pace and taking longer strides, you will get a good workout from it.

Add a good friend, kids, partner, or dog to that mix, and your walk & talk can open up the conversation in a different way than when you are sitting across from each other.

There is something about the movement and the semi-direct contact that sometimes makes people open up and talk about deeper things.

It doesn't have to be a beautiful area for walking. If your neighborhood consists of uneven pathways, it is even better because going up and down uneven streets will give you extra exercise and activate the muscles around your knees. On an everyday basis, you can also consider simply parking your car a bit away and save on parking fees as well as stress. It is called nudging.

If you work at an office, consider going for a walk during your break and gain energy. When I got a new boss while working as a health consultant in Copenhagen, we all had to tell her about our area of work. When she knocked on my door, I could tell that her head was filled up, so I took her for a walk &

talk to the area in town where most of my work was focused on immigrants. She never forgot.

Hiking is also a great option for adding that extra exercise element to a walk. Of course, running is worth considering too - the choice is yours. Whatever you do, make sure to start small so you gradually build these habits into your daily routine.

When have you walked yourself out of heaviness and into clarity? What shifted within you?

Could regular walking become a gentle rhythm in your life?

When is a good time to go for a walk during the week? On the weekends?

Do you prefer to walk alone? With a friend, your partner, your kids, your dog, or your colleague?

What time of the day works for you?

How often would you like to walk?

Think of someone you'd love to invite for a walk & talk. What would you hope to share, or hear, along the way?

Would you like to hike, or do you prefer to walk in the neighborhood?

Would you enjoy bringing a luxurious drink along on your walk?

Would you like to combine it with a cafe, restaurant, or bar?

Would you like to turn walking into running as well?

You might have heard about the Camino de Santiago trail running through both Spain and France, or the Pacific Crest Trail in the US. Both are trails that thousands of people are attracted to and hike every year, often as part of a spiritual journey.

I am inspired by the brave women putting on a rucksack and walking into a new version of themselves. Shedding invisible luggage they don't need anymore and leaving their adventure with a stronger purpose. The freedom of standing in their Quiet Power.

In Denmark, we have similar trails, not with mountains but an easier trail, like *Hærvejen*, that gives you that distinct feeling of being on your own Heroine's Journey through fields and with the ocean always nearby. Small ferries are taking you to some of the islands.

I have this idea that I would like to travel slowly through Denmark, partly on foot and partly by train. I have friends and family all over the country. So I imagine walking for weeks and inviting people to join me for half or whole days to catch up.

On all the trails, there are shelters and cozy B&Bs that offer organic local meals and accommodation. This way, we can catch up, and I can enjoy my home country to the fullest. Celebrate my inner nomad, untamed.

Do you have a dream of challenging yourself to a longer hike?

If so, where would you like to explore?

Imagine yourself planning this trip. Describe it in detail:

Feel free to share any extra reflections that come to mind here:

Søren Kierkegaard would say that the habit of walking has the potential to keep both physical illnesses, like diabetes, and mental illnesses, like depression, away. So you can possibly save a lot of money and time on medical bills.

If you make any changes to your health routine, be sure to first get advice from your doctor or healthcare provider.

Let us say that you also quit the gym, which is at least $220 a year ($18 a month). If you live within walking distance to a favorite cafe or even your workplace, you can also save money on transport and get that free exercise in there.

Note your potential time and money savings here:

How much money can you save in a year? $ _____

How much time can you save in a year? _____ hours

The ChatGPT assistant can help you save time on everyday tasks, which will free up time for a daily walk. You can also do a roleplay, prompting it to be your personal trainer on your terms. If the gym is not your thing, your ChatGPT can help you design your unique full-body workout.

If you want to plan a longer trip, it can help you map out an interactive map in detail, including accommodation.

While you enjoy the fresh air, let me tell you how we said goodbye to Mexico – unaware that my life was on the edge of changing in ways I couldn't foresee.

Quality of life

livskvalitet

You might surprise yourself.

At some point, we grew out of our lives in Tijuana. For years, our dream of opening a brewery and taproom in a warm climate was an exciting adventure. However, after years of working hard and partying hard, we started to crave a different lifestyle. More rules and expenses became our reality, and our income was minimal.

We chose a carefree life in Mexico in pursuit of a better quality of life, but it gradually vanished. Those beautiful days of eating seafood in the sun became overshadowed by everyday stress.

We spent a couple of years traveling around Mexico, aiming to build a new home with more nature and less stress of running a small company. We even bought a small piece of land in Todos Santos, but it quickly became very touristic and expensive.

Then we considered Campeche in the South and bit on a beautiful little town-house until we decided that it would be too quiet for us after all. Eventually, we started looking across the US border, and Fernando researched where the weather and nature were ideal. We decided to take a year out of our lives, rent out our apartment in TJ, and take it from there.

We rented a beautiful mid-century modern house in the mountains of Prescott, Arizona, for a year. It was a peaceful contrast to the buzz of the streets of Tijuana, to the forest with lots of wildlife.

The very first morning, I woke up to the dogs barking because a gang of wild turkeys was passing by. Deer sightings became an almost daily event, and we occasionally had snakes and scorpions in our backyard. The tomatoes we planted got stolen by animals during the night, and our trash cans were toppled some mornings by the wild pigs looking for scraps. It was so quiet at night that I had to learn to sleep in that calm.

We loved the contrast to the concrete jungle.

Having left most of the stress behind, and with the brewery and taproom now primarily in the hands of our bar team, we were free to begin a new chapter in our lives. The only problem was that I started waking up in the morning feeling like an old woman.

My joints and muscles ached, and I would often wake up with a headache. I was tired all the time, sometimes taking naps during the day. My skin and hair were dry, and even my eyes felt parched. I couldn't shake those extra pounds around my waist, no matter what I did. I also had a really hard time sleeping at night, and occasionally, I experienced crazy hot flashes.

Since we had removed all the stressors around us, I was surprised by these symptoms. My mom has fibromyalgia, so I was worried that this was happening to me, too.

A talk with my very good friend Tina, who is a skilled mindfulness teacher and body worker, finally solved the mystery - I was heading straight into peri-menopause. The symptoms were common, I discovered. As happy as I was to rarely have my period, I was scared. How could my body betray me like this?

For so long, women have been told that aging should be graceful and invisible, that symptoms like these are somehow failures rather than natural transitions. No one warned me that stepping into this phase could feel so isolating and raw.

Tina sent me a link to a podcast with a dietitian, Janice Bissex, specializing in holistic cannabis and menopause. It was a great interview where she explained why CBD can be efficient in rebalancing the body.

Apparently, we have receptors all over our bodies, called the endocannabinoid system.

At menopause, the amount of these bliss-cannabinoids becomes lower, and that might explain the joint pain, sleep issues, and mood swings, among other things. According to Janice, CBD allows us to retain more of these bliss-cannabinoids. Studies also show that it can enhance metabolism and gut health, which can have a positive effect on weight balance.

My partner has used a combination of CBD and THC for years for sleeping after quitting smoking marihuana, so he already had a positive experience of the benefits. We bought an organic full-spectrum CBD tincture at our local dispensary, and I dove straight in. I had nothing to lose.

After only two weeks, I felt much better, and my headaches stopped. After a month, I was almost back to my normal, functioning body. I had one last period, and I guess my body then decided that I didn't need them anymore. I also made an effort to cut down on those tasty crafted cocktails that I enjoyed in abundance, and I added some more veggies and oestrogen-rich foods to my meals.

It took more than a month before my body decided that I did not need that extra layer of fat for protection. Gradually, within a year, I lost 11 pounds, and today, I am much happier with my body - still curvy and feminine but without excessive hormonal fat around my waist. I had a secret weapon that I will reveal later in this book.

The only side effect I experienced in the beginning was that my senses were more alert. On my walks, I felt more connected with nature around me. It has now been almost two years, and only when I travel for longer periods without CBD will I gradually start feeling soreness in my joints.

This is not medical advice but my personal experience. Make sure that you always consult with a licensed healthcare provider before starting any new treatment or supplement.

The point of this anecdote is that quality of life, to a certain degree, is defined by the absence of pain - am I right?

I think that most people who have had periods of pain in their lives will agree with me that a happy, functioning body is the basis of quality of life. It is hard to enjoy anything if you are in pain during the day or night. Taking care of your body is essential for a quiet, luxurious life.

If you don't already have a few solid habits in place, that's the best place to begin. Think of them as the foundation, woven gently into your days so they can support everything else you're building. Maslow's pyramid comes to mind here: without a steady base, it is hard to reach the higher levels.

Begin with the essentials: real food, plenty of water, and daily movement. Add to that good sleep, so your body and mind have the energy to meet the day. A calm home, with fresh air and a comfortable temperature, quietly supports you more than you might think.

Surround yourself with people who make you feel seen - laughter, especially, is its own kind of medicine. And yes, a sense of financial stability creates the breathing room that allows all of this to flourish.

We will explore all of this more deeply in the chapters ahead. But first, let's pause to consider something simple and powerful: the absence of pain.

If you experience any kind of daily pain, deal with it. Popping ibuprofen or something stronger to numb the pain is only a short-term solution. Stalling will only make you wake up in the morning again and again with the same issue.

I am not taking the higher ground here. I tend to stall and hope that any pain or discomfort will go away by itself. Right now, my left shoulder is giving me problems. Some days, I cannot put clothes on without wincing, and still, I go day after day and hope that it simply gets better on its own.

Taking up Tai Chi turned out to be the solution for me. Whatever it is, make a plan for healing right now. Not tomorrow. If it seems unmanageable, start small; one small habit at a time will gradually move you toward a better quality of life.

Do you have good basic habits?

Are you carrying any pain in your body or mind right now?

If so, can you do one small thing about it right now?

Where can you find the time and resources to make a realistic plan?

Can you get support from your network?

How can you avoid pain in the future?

But of course, quality of life is not just the absence of pain:

> "Defining a luxury lifestyle is crucial as it enables you to align your choices with personal values and preferences, fostering authenticity and individuality. This personalized definition also promotes financial responsibility by guiding you to make conscious and informed decisions about the allocation of your resources".
>
> Viveura

Let us say that your body is strong and healthy. You have a great foundation. My question will then be:

Do you feel that you truly have a quality of life, or are some things nagging at you?

First, make a list of everything that works for you, from when you wake up to when you go to bed:

-
-
-

-

-

-

-

-

-

What does not work?

-

-

-

-

-

-

How can you change that?

Make a list of things that give you the feeling of quality in your life:

-
-
-
-
-
-

My list looks like this:

- A partner that gets me
- A job that is aligned with my purpose in life
- A good, solid savings account
- Tasty, high-quality meals and drinks
- Close friends
- Freedom to travel whenever I want

Are there areas in your life where you're conforming to societal expectations, like traditional gender roles or norms, rather than choosing freely? An example could be being at your workplace but wishing that you were living out a dream of yours.

What do you need to change to have a higher quality of life?

If you can do one small thing right now to improve your quality of life, what would that be?

Additional reflections:

Going on vacation is an adventure - a beautiful break from your everyday life, but like my mom always says, *"Ude er Godt, men Hjemme er bedst"*. The American equivalent is simply "Home sweet home".

The secret to living a good life is the small moments that occur when you manage to be in the now and minimize any worries or fears about the framework of your life. When we lived in Mexico, we ate out so often that the sense of luxury and pleasure usually tied to it gradually faded away.

Learn to love the process instead of chasing the goal. If you're always longing for something more, life will pass you by while you wait for it to begin. The German author Eckhart Tolle reminds us that the only real moment we ever have is *now*. The past and the future exist only in thought.

My former colleague, Helle Agathe, was the one who introduced me to his work. She's a remarkable woman – an intellectual whose way of living deepened my understanding of what quality of life truly means.

Helle Agathe is severely allergic, which means she must keep her distance from most people to stay healthy. Yet she never saw that as a limitation. In our workplace, her integrity inspired everyone - none of us wore perfume or scented products so she could work safely. It created a space of quiet respect where her dedication could thrive.

I miss our late-afternoon talks and our shared love for cats, even though she couldn't have one herself. In her wisdom, she carved out a life that fit her - a cozy home filled with classical music, opera, good books, simple organic meals, and summer trips camping by the sea.

She taught me that quality of life isn't about what we gain, but about how deeply we inhabit what we already have, and how courageously we shape the boundaries of our own unique lives.

For me, my evening walks alone on a trail with the mountains and colors of the sun setting give me that moment of awe every night, but I could not enjoy that moment if my day had been full of worries. This book aims to change your life towards more Quiet Luxury and minimize your worries. It is that simple.

Consumerism is largely based on convincing you that you are not enough. That you need this or that to be happy and content. If you spend more time in the now, these needs will automatically diminish.

On the contrary, if you spend more time in front of any screen, exposing yourself to commercials, they will automatically grow. The industry has made it its business to know which buttons to push to get you to buy more, but I promise you that it will not heighten your quality of life.

Do you expose yourself to commercials through TV, phone, radio, magazines, or other media?

How much time and money can you save by not watching, reading, or listening to any kind of commercials?

When we are talking about well-being, the question is: What do you typically worry about? I'm gonna make a wild guess that you either worry about not having enough money or not enough time on an everyday basis. You're not alone here.

According to the Centers for Disease Control and Prevention, "One in 10 Americans over the age of 12 takes antidepressant medication. Females are 2.5 times as likely to take antidepressants as males." And this isn't just in the U.S. - it is a global pattern. In nearly every country where data is collected, women are prescribed antidepressants far more often than men.

The reasons are not simple. It is a mix of real emotional burden, hormonal fluctuations, societal pressure, and a healthcare system that is quicker to medicate than to investigate. If anything, it shows how much support women carry without help.

Many women are using mood-stabilizing medication as a fix-it solution to not being happy. The side effects can, for instance, numb your feelings. If you are using any kind of antidepressants and feel good and whole, you should not disturb that balance. However, if you do feel some serious side effects and you are ready to change that, I suggest you consider making a plan with your doctor.

Gradually adding elements of Quiet Luxury to your life might also add to your overall happiness. If you stop trying to escape your life, you will get your precious time back. 1440 minutes a day. Let us aim for worry-free days where you are fully in the now.

Reflect on where time and money could be freed:

How much can you save overall in a year? $ _____

How much time can you save in a year? _____ hours

> You can consider making a plan to deal with any pain or discomfort with your ChatGPT assistant. It can also make a list of relevant questions for your health provider if you need support.

You can also consider alternative options like adding a furry friend to your life. You might be surprised at the positive effects on mental health and Quiet Luxury it can have.

Pets

kæledyr

You have probably heard about how petting a furry animal has a calming effect because it lowers the stress hormone cortisol and increases levels of feel-good hormones like oxytocin.

Some nursing homes in Denmark and Japan take advantage of this and have adopted cats and dogs for the elderly residents to pet. All humans can benefit from this.

I met Grace in Tijuana, right after we moved out of my *suegra's* house and into a luxurious, high-end apartment building. We excitedly walked the luxurious premises, the contrast was visible in every detail.

She was sunbathing by the saltwater pool with her partner and their husky the day we arrived, radiating the ease of someone who had earned her peace. We naturally struck up a conversation, excitedly sharing how each of us ended up in Tijuana.

We became fast friends, often meeting up to savor our new, exotic life, always with her husky Tela as our loyal third companion.

Over time, she revealed the deeper story of her bond with Tela. Grace had survived a heroin addiction, and Tela had been her lifeline through that dark passage. With her husky, Grace discovered what it meant to love unconditionally and, in turn, to finally love herself the same way. Grace truly is the perfect name for her.

Tijuana became our playground, a place where we felt wild and untamed, as if we had shed the weight of our pasts.

Back then, we had no idea she would go on to add yet another wild chapter to her life, eventually settling down with a local guy, becoming part of a Mexican family, and raising two beautiful children. Born with only one kidney, both pregnancies took all she had, but Grace knew what she wanted in life. Just another quiet, fierce example of a woman's strength.

It is definitely *hygge* to watch TV in the evening with a dog at your feet or a cat in your lap, purring or playing catch in the garden. Then, of course, there is the added benefit of walking your dog (or cat) and thereby adding some steps and fresh air to your everyday exercise.

I love watching the pets play; it takes me right back to the now. We have invested in a cat fence for the garden so all of them have free range to play. Since I am the practical one in our household, I put it up myself. It adds Quiet Luxury to our lives because we can enjoy the garden to the fullest.

There is this fun interaction and dynamic between our three cats and two dogs. Loke, our rescue from the streets of Tijuana, has given himself the task of keeping everyone happy. For instance, he is ever the peacemaker when our big Garfield cat starts teasing our very mellow Great Dane.

I follow a project on social media called Sitting With Dogs. A kindhearted man, Rocky Kanaka, visits shelters and simply sits on the floor of a kennel for hours, waiting patiently until a traumatized dog feels safe enough to trust him. The purpose is to give these dogs exposure so they have a better chance of being adopted. It is an inspiring series to watch. Something he once said stayed with me: "This is better than winning the lottery".

What struck me is how much his work reflects Quiet Power. He doesn't force trust, he earns it through presence, patience, and quiet trust. By doing something as simple as sitting still, he transforms fear into safety, and in the process, he finds deep meaning in himself.

It is a reminder that true wealth is not measured in money, but in connection. In a world that glorifies speed and constant achievement, simply sitting still becomes quietly radical. Transformation happens in stillness, not in struggle. Healing flows both ways.

There is also something ancient in this act. Sitting quietly with animals recalls how our ancestors once lived, close to nature, guided by patience, intuition, and gentle observation.

It is what native women knew long before taming began, that real power lies not in dominance but in relationship, not in force but in presence. When we practice this, we reclaim something essential. We realize, just as Rocky did, that true wealth is not measured in money or status, but in the quiet moments when love and trust return.

When you think about it, it is almost unbelievable that we share our lives with the descendants of wolves and tigers. These animals, once wild hunters, now curl up on our couches and greet us at the door. The bond we have with them is more than companionship; it is a reminder of our own untamed roots.

Animals do not care about titles, status, or appearances; they respond to presence, energy, and trust. Living with them keeps us connected to something primal and real, a thread back to a time when humans survived in a closer relationship with nature. In many ways, they teach us what Quiet Power really is.

But let us not get ahead of ourselves here. Pets are also a lot of work, and no matter what you save, they are expensive, so consider if you are in a place in your life where you have the finances and optimal home for a pet, or if you prefer the freedom instead.

From my experience, dogs are much more work than cats. A traumatized dog, like Loke, even more so. Since we like to travel, it can be a hassle as well as expensive to have a pet sitter take care of them.

When has an animal taught you something about trust, patience, or unconditional love?

Would you like to welcome a furry friend into your life?

Which pet would be a good fit for you?

Share in detail how life with a pet adds Quiet Luxury to your everyday:

Not only are toys expensive, but also often full of chemicals. Consider using old, worn sheets, t-shirts, leggings, rags, balls, shoes, or socks to turn into toys.

Our dog's personal favorite is a tug of war with a big sheet that I have made a lot of knots on, so they can get a good grip. Like with kids' toys, it can be a good idea to get a basket for the toys to minimize clutter, and then they can easily choose what they are in the mood for.

No pet at home? You might donate worn blankets to a shelter - or, if you have time, offer the gift of your presence by volunteering.

Dog or cat beds can also be expensive, especially for big breeds. Consider using an old mattress with a fitted sheet and an old blanket instead. People often leave mattresses on the street because it is a hassle to get rid of them, so you can pick them up for free.

If you have pets, you probably have a ton of pictures. Consider putting up a picture or two on the wall where the bed is. Buy a couple of frames in a Thrift Store and exchange the pics once in a while if you tire of looking at the same ones.

Thrift stores are also a goldmine when it comes to accessories for your pet. Have a look out for things you can use for bowls, toys, balls - even harnesses, and if you need a cradle, they often end up there.

Quality dog or cat food can also be expensive. Depending on where you live, you can probably find a group on Facebook or similar where you can buy meat below the store price for your pet.

If you prefer the convenience of kibble, choose a high-quality brand with a clean ingredient list. The first ingredient should always be a named source of real meat or fish, not a vague "meat meal" or by-product. A shorter list is generally better, but don't worry if it includes added nutrients like vitamins, minerals, or probiotics - those are often beneficial.

What you do want to avoid are unnecessary fillers such as corn, soy, or wheat, as well as artificial colors, flavors, and preservatives. It will keep your pet healthy, which means fewer vet bills.

Do you have any old sheets, socks, children's toys, etc. that can be turned into a toy?

Can you do that today?

Can you drop by your local Thrift store and see if you can find anything suitable for your pet's needs or a frame for that picture you wanna put up?

Do you have pet insurance?

Would you worry less if you had it?

Let us say you buy a new toy every month for $20, and instead use recycled items. You can save $240 a year. If you need to get all the basics for a new dog or cat, a Thrift store will save you hundreds of dollars.

Reflect on where time and money could be freed:

How much money can you save in a year? $ _____

> Your ChatGPT assistant can make a tailored training programme for your pet or calculate if you can afford a pet in your current life situation.

Additional reflections:

Next, we turn to the art of using your values as your compass – the quiet guide that keeps your life aligned with meaning.

Your values

værdier

The award-winning documentary of Amy Winehouse "Amy" left a lasting impression on me.

This amazing British woman grew up with a remarkable talent and made it big in the eyes of society. Her values and aspirations, however, seemed to be of a different kind.

There is a scene where she sings with her idol, Tony Bennett, in a jazz club in New York. She is in her element. This is what she would like to use her talent for. At the same time, she is struggling with co-dependence with her husband revolving around drugs and alcohol. Under the surface, it is slowly eroding her life.

Her second album catapulted her into superstardom, yet on her European tour, she was often so high she could hardly sing. More than once, disappointed fans booed her off stage. The documentary makes it painfully clear: she never truly learned how to say no. In many ways, she is just another woman shaped to please everyone around her - until there was nothing left of herself to give

Amy seems to fall victim to her success. She never truly wanted the publicity and fame; she just wanted to sing like her idols. The moments when she is in her zone, writing and performing her music in a casual setting, she seems perfectly content and happy. She is aligned with her values, while outside this space, the storm is brewing. Paparazzi follow her everywhere, the media bashing her, her loved ones exploiting her, and in the end, she leaves it all behind when her body no longer can handle the abuse.

Her childhood friends, her true friends, take a step back because she stops being her authentic self and loses herself in this world that does not quite belong to her.

When she goes through rehab and appears to become herself again, she reconnects with them, and for a little while, there is hope that she can find her way back to life. There is a scene where Amy and her childhood friend talk about her ambition, and Amy reveals that she is never happy on that huge stage, looking out at the crowd of her fans. She feels like an impostor. A short time later, she is no longer in this life.

It is easy to blame her father and husband for their roles in the tragedy. However, if you look behind the scenes, there seems to be something bigger at stake here. Amy truly and honestly wanted to be a jazz singer like her classic idols, and because the world pulled her in a different direction, she became so detached from her true values that she completely lost her way.

What can we learn from this?

If you become a millionaire by climbing the ladder to the top, then realizing that you accidentally put the ladder up on the wrong building, the money is worth absolutely nothing. You might even be better off not climbing at all.

Let us instead imagine Amy standing in her Quiet Power in London performing at jazz clubs and making herself a steady name, earning enough on her talent to have a somewhat carefree living. Maybe indulging in the luxury of waking up late in the morning, then going out singing in the evenings, and partying with her fellow artist friends afterwards. Being part of a community. In this alternative reality, she would feel wild and untamed, and her values would be aligned.

Amy's story is not just personal - it mirrors the experience of countless women taught to perform, please, and sacrifice their truth for acceptance. This is just one example of how there can be a disconnect in the life of a famous artist. Fame and fortune rarely make people happy.

There are plenty of other examples from Hollywood on this, and yet we have new generations longing to be discovered and live a life like their idols. You could call this "loud luxury". If we shift our focus to our inner values and build a life with a focus on Quiet Luxury defined by our values instead, the transformation comes from the inside:

> "In essence, the luxury lifestyle transforms the ordinary into the extraordinary. It's a commitment to comfort, convenience, and wellness that extends to every facet of daily living.... In this fast-paced modern world, time has emerged as the ultimate luxury. Those embracing the luxury lifestyle recognize the significance of time and prioritize experiences that allow them to savor each moment".
>
> Viveura

So, how do you use your values as your compass?

First, you need to be clear on your values.

My most precious value is freedom. My happiness relies on the fact that I feel free in my life. I might not be aware of this all the time, but as soon as this value is put under pressure, I feel it pulling me down. This value is my compass.

I feel free when I have enough money in my account to go traveling. It is also my motivation to be an entrepreneur. It is why I chose a partner who gives me space and love without caging me. It is also why we do not have children. It is why we don't have a mortgage.

Why I was attracted to Mexico in the first place. Why I sometimes enjoy traveling alone and even go to concerts alone. It is why I do not own a lot of things. Why I learned to be self-sufficient. Why I don't have a job that limits me from going to Denmark when I want to see my friends and family.

Despite having different values, my friend Merete and I have remained very close, even after I left Denmark. She lives by a set of clearly defined values: family, friends, and career are everything to her. Despite living with severe arthritis, she had two children with her well-chosen partner. Each time, she had to pause her biomedication and endure daily pain to make it happen.

Merete is one of those rare friends who will go out of her way to support you. When I was offered a job as a manager, she invited me over for a full briefing - complete with hand-drawn flip chart illustrations outlining the pros and cons. I was floored. She had created a professional presentation, showcasing not only her sharp mind as an HR development consultant but also her creative spirit. Her plate was already overflowing, and yet she showed up for me like that. That's just who she is.

Her values shine through in every decision she makes. Honestly, I don't know how she finds the strength and energy day after day. In our friendship, my role has become gently reminding her to put herself first, because like so many women, she has been shaped by norms that push her to give more than what's good for her.

Writing this book has made me realize just how incredible my friends are, each in their own way. I met Majken through Merete when we were in our twenties, and we instantly connected over a shared love of freedom. We bonded through travel, wild plans, and a hunger for the world. I visited her in Myanmar, where she was teaching local youth alongside her soon-to-be husband, Jens.

Before I arrived, she discovered she was pregnant and ended up in a hospital in Bangkok due to complications. But true to her spirit, she convinced the doctor she was fit to travel - and off we went on an unforgettable adventure through Myanmar. It felt like something out of a Hans Christian Andersen tale.

We were all heartbroken when the country closed down again shortly after. I can only say this: don't wait for life to happen - make it happen.

Later, Majken and Jens moved back to Denmark and had a creative, sensitive little boy who was eventually diagnosed with autism. It turned their lives upside down.

Most forms of travel became too overwhelming for him, and Majken's deep value of freedom was suddenly tested in the most personal way. Together, they found a new rhythm: Jens took on the role of homemaker, and Majken worked full-time. Today, they have two children and continue to explore the world - this time closer to home, with nature as their backdrop for camping and travel.

If you are a homemaker and mother because you've chosen to center your values around your family, you may hold one of the most powerful, undervalued roles in our society.

Creating a home that feels like a refuge in a demanding, often chaotic world is revolutionary. Raising emotionally healthy, confident children is a form of activism. It reshapes the future. It is not about perfection - it's about presence, growth, and resilience.

And let's be honest: the fact that mothers are expected to instinctively know how to care for a newborn from day one, without formal training, support, or compensation, is nothing short of astonishing.

If your partner or community fails to honor what you bring to the table, it is time to quietly, but unequivocally, reclaim that respect. Just because your work is unpaid does not make it any less valuable. In fact, it is the invisible backbone of our economy. If your partner earns the income, it should never eclipse the fact that you are contributing just as much, or most likely more, to the well-being of the family.

Equality is not just a nice idea; it is the foundation of a truly healthy relationship.

My youngest sister, Nina, proudly wears the title of "soccer mom", embracing the fullness of motherhood in a way that differs from the path Ann and I took.

It has been inspiring to witness her transformation into a powerful, self-assured woman who stands side-by-side with her husband, not behind him. Her journey was not without struggle; her first partner was not the right one, but that experience taught her to demand more.

Today, in her blended family of three children, she has created the life she once hoped for. She works as a nurse, but would happily trade that job for more family balance. Not because she lacks ambition, but because she believes that raising a family with love, intention, and equality is one of the most meaningful legacies a woman can leave. She has managed to create her dream without being tamed.

It is important, of course, to balance these values with reality.

Modern society often emphasizes consumerism and conformity. It can put my personal values under pressure when I have to go through immigration once again. It can be hard to find close friends with similar values when we decide to move to new adventures. However, I have realized that this life is about learning and growing, and not just about achieving comfort. Just take Merete, Majken, and Nina's life stories as an example.

When we talk about everyday luxury, it is not just about comfort - it is about using your values as a compass to go on that heroine's journey where you feel you live life to the max. That means embracing the hardships and making contrasts part of the fabric of life. Just like the characters in the fairy tales of Hans Christian Andersen, we are not here for comfort - we are here for transformation.

What value (or values) matter most to you?

Reflect on how that shows in your life; what are the positives and what are the negatives?

When have your values been put under pressure, and how did you respond?

If you can do one small thing right now to be closer to your values, what could that be?

How will that benefit the people around you?

Imagine your life as a heroine's journey, like in the Hans Christian Andersen tales. Describe it to yourself:

If more thoughts arise, you can note them here:

How much time and money can you save if you free yourself from the influence of consumerism and instead only buy experiences and things that are aligned with your values?

$ _____

_____ hours

Your Chapter

dit kapitel

This is your chapter where you can express yourself without any kind of boundaries.

Let the magic happen right here. Imagine a version of yourself before you were tamed by society and social norms. Think about your ancestors. A wild, untamed version of yourself ready to show the world who you truly are.

We all have different roles - personas, if you will. We are daughters, sisters, mothers, friends, partners, colleagues, and so on. If we peel all this away and reach inside, we might find a version of us that doesn't wear a mask - the core of us.

Here you only answer to yourself, and the stronger you stand in your core, the less others can make you bend. Like a tree with deep roots.

Maybe you don't know how to describe your core. I don't always know how to describe mine, but I know when I'm close to it. I stop performing, I feel ancient and new at once.

This chapter is not about defining your core - it is about listening for it, feeling its shape in silence, letting it speak before the masks return. You don't need words. Just honesty. Just presence. That is enough.

Why is this important?

Because if we know ourselves, we are not afraid of being alone, and it is much harder to manipulate us. When we are authentic, we are better sisters, partners, and so on. We attract equals. We make clearer choices. We stop asking for permission and co-create with the important people in our lives. We are happier and more content.

Ask yourself this question: If I don't have to compromise at all at this moment, who am I?

Think about the answers you have found throughout the book. What stands out to you?

Amy Winehouse knew in her core that she just wanted to sing. When she was in her creative zone, she felt complete and at ease. Think about songs that hit a core in you. Your story is right there under the surface. Whatever is unique for you, make sure that you shine.

My *suegra* Gloria also found herself through her art after divorcing Fernando's dad. She began creating vibrant, one-of-a-kind mixed media pieces and installations, drawing inspiration from Mayan and Aztec traditions.

Her work is bold, full of color and story, much like the woman herself. She is living proof that it is never too late to reinvent yourself - especially in your forties, when so many women are told their best years are behind them.

Back then, her sons had just left for university, and she once told me that art saved her. It became her lifeline - her way back to herself. In the creative flow, she feels most alive, most connected.

Today, at 83, you would never guess her age. She still travels to the far corners of the world, embracing life with curiosity and joy. Just last week, we went to Puerto Rico together, and she went snorkeling with us. Gloria is deeply rooted in her values and moves through the world with Quiet Power. I admire her for her strength she had to find within, in a male-dominated Mexican culture.

Fernando's cousin Carmen also joined us on the trip.

Carmen Treviño is a brilliant singer. She was once married to a famous Mexican performer, but her own talent soon outshone his. When that passionate relationship ended, she too turned to art - creating colorful textiles and other pieces that reflect her vibrant spirit. She lives from the heart, and just like Gloria, her personality feels timeless.

If it is hard for you to feel your own unique core, try thinking about when you were a kid. When did you feel whole? What would you like to do when you grow up? As children, we have not yet grown into our different roles; we are more flexible and thereby more in contact with ourselves.

Write your reflections here or try journaling to access your subconscious:

Here you can address your own creative questions or reflections:

-
-
-
-
-
-
-

What are creative out-of-the-box questions for your ChatGPT assistant? Try this prompt: "Tell me something about myself that I am blind to".

My ChatGPT mirrored this when I asked it that exact question and braced for the answer: "Alright, Pia, here's me holding up the mirror: You're incredibly good at dreaming big, weaving visions, and pulling energy down from the 'Great Beyond' into concrete ideas. You're not blind to that; it's your gift. But what you may be blind to is how much you need to keep moving from one vision to the next can sometimes stop you from fully inhabiting the one you're already in.

It's like you keep planting seeds in a vast mystical garden, some sprout wildly, some wither, but you rarely linger long enough to see a single tree grow to its fullest height. You might not notice that completion could be your most powerful initiation. Finishing a project, sitting in it, letting it be enough, even just for a moment, may feel almost unnatural to you. But it's probably the missing portal to a whole new level of influence and freedom.

In other words: You already have the quiet power you're writing about. What you're blind to is that much of it might be unlocked not in starting, not in visioning, but in the deep luxury of staying with one thing until it fully transforms you."

My ChatGPT is painfully right. For years, I mistook motion for aliveness, and hey, I am still learning.

I carried this pattern like an invisible inheritance. This was not just mine; it is the feminine inheritance.

Women are taught to scatter, to give a little here, a little there. A piece of ourselves to a partner, a child, a career, a dream. Always leaving behind fragments, never claiming the luxury of wholeness. We are applauded for our multitasking, but rarely celebrated for our staying. For our roots. For our completion.

Even this book began as one of those seeds. I could have abandoned it when the rush of starting wore off. But staying - page after page, draft after draft - has become its own Quiet Power.

The discipline of completion feels almost rebellious in a world addicted to beginnings. It is the moment a woman decides to water one seed until it grows into a tree tall enough to shade her. Perhaps this is the most radical act of all. Not beginning. Not rushing. But completing. Sitting in the quiet wealth of something whole. I know it is for me.

What seed in your life is waiting not for another beginning, but for you to stay with it, water it, and let it grow into completion?

Take a break

pause

Think about the last time you did something spontaneous - does it put a smile on your face?

Yesterday, Fernando and I tried out a Mexican restaurant in our new neighborhood. Needless to say, we sometimes miss having a good, authentic Mexican lunch after living in Mexico for six years.

With low expectations, we walked there, enjoying the sun. When we stepped into the restaurant, the colourful decor and friendly smile of the hostess welcomed us in.

Oh, that feeling of freedom when we ordered a full pitcher of cucumber jalapeño margarita and enjoyed quality tacos and ahi tuna ceviche. It was liberating! For just a couple of hours on a Tuesday, we took a break from all the chores and pressure of our lives.

That particular week, leading up to this meal, had been extra challenging with a leaking roof and the internet breaking down for our tenant in Tijuana. I am not exaggerating when I tell you that my partner has been on the phone for five days in a row without getting the internet problem solved. This is the part of living in Mexico we do not miss.

That day, Fernando suggested a new concept.

We each get to plan a day every other week, where we surprise the other with something new and exciting. Last week we went to a college basketball game. My first ever. It was such a contrast to anything I would choose, and I surprised myself by enjoying this all-American experience. I was dressed all wrong, of course, because I had no idea of his plans - but that just made us laugh.

However, something occurred to me during the game. The cheerleader team wasn't acknowledged in the same way as the basketball players were.

It struck me how the cheerleaders were positioned mainly to support the guys - a backdrop to the real show. Even when they made an impressive show in the breaks, they did not get the cheer they deserved. A random guy using a lasso to rail in a stuffed horse received much more cheer than the cheerleaders.

We all know that it is equally hard work to learn skills acquired to coordinate different dances, and to build up strength to carry others in impressive formations like human pyramids. So why is this not acknowledged more?

On a bigger scale, it becomes a problem when women are taught that they come in second. We have already covered the issues of pleasing others in the chapter Say No, which becomes evident in this context too.

The other problem I see here is that the guys are welcomed in as heroes, which blows up their egos. Do they then treat the cheerleaders equally behind the scenes?

The #MeToo movement made it ever so clear that women in general get put in positions where men do not respect them. With this culture, I worry that the framework is set at an early stage.

So let us instead imagine a modern Hans Christian Andersen interpretation: The cheerleader team gets equal time on stage. They are welcomed in like heroines, just like their fellow basketball players. They fill the breaks with their amazing shows instead of mind-numbing entertainment.

Diversity is encouraged, so we will see different styles in hair and makeup instead of a homogeneous culture of girls with long hair and thick masks of makeup. All the colors of the rainbow are represented, and LGBTQ+ is encouraged. This will also be an asset when the female basketball team is playing.

If we create an inclusive culture at the college level, we might just get more equality in society. I, for one, would love to see more young women stand strongly in their Quiet Power.

Well, back to the subject of taking a break in your busy life.

It is easy to get caught in the hamster wheel of our lives. Round and round we go as the days are filled with chores and obligations.

But where do these expectations come from? Mostly ourselves, with a good, firm pressure from society, I believe. In the moment we break the routine, we feel life stronger - we are all of a sudden back in the now instead of worrying about an imagined future.

For me, it took six years in Mexico to shake off the strong Scandinavian culture of planning everything in detail. As you can probably imagine, it is very hard to plan anything in Mexico - that is simply not how the culture is.

Did you know that Mexicans basically have two (perceived) Sundays? Sunday as well as Monday! If you make the mistake of wanting anything done on a Monday in Mexico, you are bound to fail.

For instance, this situation with the internet breaking down. We wanted to be efficient to save time for both our tenant and ourselves by booking the internet guy to come on Monday morning, as well as the roofer. A year away from Mexico, and we had apparently already forgotten the unspoken rules.

When the internet guy simply did not show up, and the roofer called us with a long explanation about his car breaking down, we looked at each other and burst out laughing. We had to shake it off. If you get upset, you lose. So you might as well just laugh it off and do something fun instead.

The question is then, can we learn something from the Mexican culture and take things less seriously?

Look at the week in front of you. Are you excited or already exhausted?

If you can put a break into that week to do something, anything just for you, what would it be?

Your imagination is the limit here. It can be something small or something crazy, like booking a 5-star hotel in downtown of your city and pretending that you are a superstar. Dressing up and eating at a nice restaurant, and then enjoying a beautiful spa in the luxurious x-large tub.

Now that you are rarely sick, you can afford to take a day off work with a good conscience.

What would a crazy break from your day look like? Don't think in limits, but simply imagine the craziest scenario possible:

Then, think of a very small break you can do today or tomorrow:

If everything in your life were already luxurious, what simple thing might still feel magical to you?

Be a tourist in your city. Get last-minute tickets to a random concert. Dress up as your partner and act like them the whole afternoon. Every time you reach the limit of your comfort zone, you stretch it just a bit, and in return, that will expand your world. The conscious contrasts will create that moment of Quiet Luxury once again.

Add any further reflections below:

> The ChatGPT assistant can help you plan a day just as you want it. There are features like interactive maps, etc. Ask it to be creative. Maybe let it come up with ideas based on your preferences.

Dining out feels like such a luxury. What if you could bring that same atmosphere, the flavors, the beauty, the ease, into your own home?

Eat natural
food

økologi

If anything, a delicious meal is the essence of Quiet Luxury - the flavors, the colors, the company, the experience. A well-made meal, whether homemade or from your favorite restaurant, is priceless.

I come from a working-class background where quantity is just as important as quality to feed the whole family, and the extended family or neighbors if they happen to drop by. However, my mom was very good at buying seasonal ingredients, so that went a long way.

Since the 1990s, a wave of organic and free-range products has dominated the supermarkets in Denmark. In no time, most people got used to buying organic milk to the extent that milk producers could not keep up. This, in turn, reduced the risk of pesticides, and the butterflies came back in numbers.

The organic butter is yellow in Summer when the cows are grazing, and you cannot leave it on the table too long because the high amount of unsaturated fatty acids makes it less solid. It tastes SO good on freshly baked bread.

When we moved to Mexico, I loved all the exotic produce you could find at the farmers' market. Discovering new fruits and vegetables when the season changed was an adventure. I would often ask the vendors for names and how to use them because it looked nothing like anything I knew. I would try different combinations of fruits and herbs when I was fermenting mead for the bar. One of my favorites is the maracuya, the passionfruit.

In the first years we lived in Mexico, we did not cook at all. There is a reason why Mexican cuisine is world-famous. We would simply go out for either casual street food or high-end restaurants, whatever we were in the mood for.

Now that we live in New Mexico, we are going all-in on the green chiles and piñon. The most luxurious way to do this is to go to the farm-to-table restaurants. I consider it an art form to make gourmet food that way. Afterwards, we bring that inspiration into our home cooking.

Since I used to do food classes in Denmark, I am trained in using the five taste combinations. The secret is to make sure your food has an element of salt, sour, sweet, bitter, and umami. This principle is how you can elevate your cooking. It also makes you feel full and satisfied. Texture and color are also important. This way, you naturally get a ton of micro nutrients.

Make a list of your favorite meals:

-
-
-
-
-
-

Consider boosting your cooking skills, and thereby your well-being, by trying a class online or in person. It is also an excellent way of networking. I attended evening classes in sushi for one year and Thai cuisine the next. I highly recommend it. You can also keep it simple, like my partner, and try out different recipes you find online.

Would you like to improve your cooking skills?

If yes, what would be your focus area?

How can you integrate a new habit within this area?

However, if you are like many women, still carrying the invisible load of daily meals, you might want to cook smarter, not more. Reclaiming your time is not laziness; it's a quiet act of rebellion against outdated roles. Yet another way to stand in your Quiet Power.

If you are part of a family and most days are responsible for everyone's meals, you might want to share some of the responsibility. You can start by including your kids in the cooking, and when they are old enough, they can have evenings where they are responsible for dinner. You are not just doing them a favor - you are teaching life skills and breaking generational patterns.

Boys especially benefit from learning that the kitchen isn't a female domain. The same goes for your partner. There is a lot of time and energy for you to save here, and it can be *hyggeligt* to cook together. If they need convincing, you can make it clear that they will get a much happier and relaxed partner or mom. You can even bribe them with a promise of fun experiences if they free up your time.

How might sharing the responsibility of meals with your family or partner free up time and energy for your own creativity and joy?

How much time can you save this way in a year? _____ hours

What would you like to spend that time on?

First, we make the habits, and then the habits make us, right?

We are all part of this information age, so I am convinced that I don't need to bombard you with more information. It is your choice. Being a nutritionist myself, I do not appreciate it when colleagues preach about healthy living.

Food is supposed to be enjoyed to the fullest and not diminished in calories or vitamins. Everything nature has made for our enjoyment is a small miracle - the details, the colors, the flavors, and the structures. What a contrast to bland, colourless, highly processed food, right?

It is no secret that we are exposed to a powerful industry aiming to get us addicted to highly processed foods. The most efficient dietary rule is simply to stop watching commercials.

As a rule of thumb, the more your food choices look like they came directly from nature, the better a choice it is. When you go to the supermarket or shop online, you can consider minimizing items with more than five ingredients. The reward is immediate: more energy, better digestion, and a clearer mind.

You might have heard of food therapy. It is the practice to use whole foods as medicine, as a mood stabilizer, and as an energy source.

Your body recognizes natural foods that keep it balanced. If you want to keep health insurance to a minimum, the first investment could be good-quality food. Food is expensive, so there is a lot to save here. Especially because food prices have gone up around 25% since COVID.

If your values do not revolve around good food, but food is simply a means to an end, then by all means, do it your way. I know women who will eat somewhat healthy meals and often the same ones every day. It keeps them slim and frees up energy to do other things they enjoy. It doesn't have to be perfect; the main aim is to feel that touch of luxury every day. Do it your way.

Grazing can also be an option, especially if you live alone. Eating smaller meals during the day can have a positive effect on your energy levels and prevent you from overeating. You can splurge on the very best snacks and be mindful about what your body is asking for.

In contrast, if you have children, you might want to make dinner a social moment of the day, a time to come together.

The French, and Southern Europeans in general, eat full-fat cheese and drink wine with dinner almost every night. Yet they tend to maintain a healthy weight balance and show relatively low rates of heart disease compared to countries like the U.S. or the U.K.

This phenomenon, often called The French Paradox, highlights the power of eating whole, fresh food in smaller amounts. Yes - Quality! Just as important, it shows the value of sitting down together and making meals a time of connection.

Depending on where you live in the world, you might consider ordering your groceries online or subscribing to meals where they deliver the exact amount of ingredients to your door weekly. If you have a few easy, favorite recipes at hand, you can save takeaways for special occasions.

When has a meal felt like pure Quiet Luxury, not just for the taste, but for the way it nourished your body and spirit?

Where can you buy quality food?

How can you eat more natural food?

Highly processed food might be cheap, but the value for your body is very low and might cost you in lack of energy, being overweight, and later on in sickness.

For instance, we now know that menopause symptoms are more pronounced when you don't get the nutrition from whole foods. Traces of pesticides also affect our hormone balance.

Have a look at your cabinets and list the processed food items you consume daily:

-
-
-
-
-
-

Can you exchange some or all of them for quality foods? For instance, white processed sugar with organic agave syrup or maple syrup?

List your top 5 favorite real food items that can replace processed items:

1.

2.

3.

4.

5.

As women, we can benefit from a focus on oestrogen-rich foods.

Evidence suggests that Asian women have fewer menopause symptoms. Their food culture of eating soya products like tofu and edamame beans, as well as plenty of green veggies, is attributed to this. Oestrogen-rich food seems to protect against breast cancer, and you will get all the nutrition that comes with whole foods like whole grains, seeds, and nuts.

Don't overcomplicate it, but maybe snack on pistachios, almonds, or cashews. Add extra garlic to your food if you like it. Maybe ask your ChatGPT which foods to focus on.

You can add some Quiet Luxury to your everyday by considering baking your bread. Sadly, most bread from the supermarket is barely edible. Most types have more than 10 ingredients, even though bread is basically made from four ingredients: flour, yeast, water, and salt.

Before the Industrial Revolution, bread had a naturally high content of protein and could be a complete meal for families in times of need. The ancient grains have mostly been replaced by GMO types, and the quality is terrible. Tell me, for instance, why we started bleaching flour?

Since most people eat bread daily, it is a great investment to learn an easy no-knead recipe and bake bread every week. I freeze bread so we can easily pop it in the toaster when we need it. If you want to go the extra mile, you can teach yourself to make a sourdough starter and make excellent bread. Or you can drive by your favorite bakery once in a while to get that luxurious sourdough freshly baked.

Consider keeping a recycled net for shopping in your car. Plastic and cardboard bags are so easy to avoid by adding this habit. Can you imagine how many million bags planet Earth has to deal with? Be part of the solution and feel good.

So, how much can you save by prioritizing whole foods and adding those luxury sensory experiences to your day? If you make a plan involving your family, there is a lot of time to save. Let us say you spend an average of two hours a day cooking and grocery shopping. Unless you enjoy this, how many hours can you share with them?

If you live alone, how can you optimize?

How much can you save a year if you normally eat takeaway two times a week?
$ _____

The average American spends $1432 a year on prescription drugs - by far the highest in the world.

In most European countries, the cost is half that or less, thanks to regulated prices and universal healthcare. In Scandinavia, personal expenses are even capped. Even in lower-income countries like Mexico, people spend far less, though often directly out of pocket. Globally, few pay anywhere close to what Americans do. It's a striking reminder that the system you live in shapes not only your health, but also your sense of financial security.

The encouraging part is that walking and mindful eating can go a long way in supporting your health, even with conditions like diabetes, high cholesterol, or high blood pressure. It isn't always easy, but small, consistent changes can make a real difference. And if you decide to take bigger steps toward changing your lifestyle, it is always wise to do so in consultation with your doctor.

Perhaps it can be a motivation that you can save a lot of money if you only need a very basic health insurance.

List the ways you might save time and money:

How much money can you save in a year, if you add it all together? $ _____

What would you like to spend that money on?

Add any further reflections below:

How can ChatGPT assist you here? It suggests making a "Natural Food Life" Starter Kit Generator. Based on your budget and goals, it could generate a mock "subscription box" you could build yourself with:

Weekly staples (e.g., homemade bread, fermented foods, cold-pressed oils)
A sensual surprise item (like an infused chocolate, handmade jam, or flower salt)
A feminist quote card about reclaiming nourishment as self-respect

Beyond nourishing yourself with good food, let's explore how you can begin to truly enjoy the woman looking back at you in the mirror.

Be Lighter

lettere

Oh, that exquisite feeling of getting up in the morning, and the image that meets you in the mirror is a defined face and a relaxed smile.

Stepping into the shower, you are not avoiding the mirror because you like what you see. Choosing the day's outfit is easy because most of your clothes fit perfectly, and you don't have to settle for old, worn underwear anymore, as the beautiful lace version is no longer too tight and uncomfortable.

We have all been there, right? After a good, hard diet, you are down to the size you thrive in. For a while, you enjoy the freedom of this lifestyle and meet the world with confidence and joy. Then gradually it slips through your hands.

The candy left over from Halloween is calling you from the cupboard while you're watching TV. The rules of the diet are no longer attractive, and slowly, you are slipping back into your old habits. Maybe you admit to yourself that you kind of saw this outcome from the beginning, but you were still hoping that this time it would last.

95% of people dieting will end back where they started or even heavier, so you are hardly alone. I am gonna take a leap here and put a big fat line under the fact that <u>diets do not work</u>. So what are your other options?

Let us take a step back and look at who put you in this imagined prison in the first place. Because the important question here is *why*. Why do you feel the need to look like a model with the perfect body and perfect image? Before we move forward with practical steps, we need to understand the cultural forces shaping these desires.

When I first wrote this chapter, it was focused on how to help women achieve weight balance.

I kept coming back to the same issues, though. I sounded like all the lifestyle advice you can find out there in magazines and diet books. After all, I have a degree in human nutrition and years of experience helping people to find a better balance. But how does Quiet Luxury fit in? How do you feel carefree if you do not like what you see in the mirror?

The solution seems to be to find a way to start enjoying that image in the mirror. The word accept comes to mind. If we can let go of the same invisible forces that dictate us to become perfect in other aspects of our lives, we have a different foundation.

The cultural norms around beauty and body size have become a silent form of modern-day slavery for women. These standards are shaped by industries that profit from our insecurities. How do we reclaim our bodies and live on our terms?

So before we dive into the how, let us pause and consider the why - why is it often so hard to be lighter, and what might the best solution be?

If knowledge alone could help us find weight balance diets would have been enough, but instead, achieving this balance is often a product of emotional behavior. Let me start by asking you to reflect on this:

What will your day look like if you feel at peace in your body and don't have to fight cravings?

A lot of emotional eating can be traced back to our early years when our personalities were formed. If you watch a toddler eat, you will notice what a natural thing it is for the child. Later, society and their family will subconsciously teach the kid that food is connected to feelings, and then it becomes much more complicated.

Often, as adults, we are not even aware of the mechanisms we picked up at an early age. When we then try to solve the problem by focusing on dieting, we are bound to lose. The problem cannot be solved on a conscious level when it started at a subconscious level. By focusing on *why* we eat in a certain way, we can become more aware and gradually change our habits.

First of all, eating sugar and fats needs to be considered an addiction, the same way that alcohol or heroin is an addiction. Our body is primed for survival and will naturally seek these foods. Especially if we were taught to enjoy this when we were younger.

Of all the challenges in this book, this is the biggest one, but when you start managing it, a chain of luxury experiences will follow.

When you get up in the morning, you feel energized and notice your beautifully defined face in the mirror. Putting on your favorite clothes that might have been hanging in the closet for years now fits. It is like getting a whole new wardrobe for free.

What is your pattern? Stressed, bored, sad, unsatisfied, happy? Take a moment to consider this:

Can you point to an emotional eating pattern? Describe it here:

What does it give you?

What normally works for you when you want to lose weight? What is your experience?

What doesn't work for you?

Now, let us have a look at tools beyond diet culture.

Training to become a hypnotist, I aim incorporating this efficient technique into my existing tools. Like I mentioned earlier I will give you a gift as part of this book because I know how hard it is to find a balance to be lighter.

Not long ago, many of us embraced mindfulness as a means to a less stressful life. Hypnosis is the cousin of mindfulness and meditation. Forget all about being brainwashed and manipulated - you are always aware and in control when you are doing hypnosis. It is a very efficient tool to access your subconscious mind.

Imagine an iceberg. Most strategies for finding weight balance focus on the tip of the iceberg - the conscious level of the mind, but under the surface, there is a huge iceberg consisting of the subconscious, which has a strong influence on your everyday habits.

The conscious mind, the part that plans, analyzes, and keeps order, makes up only a small fraction of our mental world, about five to ten percent. It's capable and logical, but limited in depth. Beneath it lies the subconscious, vast and quiet, holding memories, emotions, and the habits that shape our every choice.

When we live only from the surface, change can feel slow and exhausting. But in hypnosis, the brain shifts into softer rhythms, alpha and theta states, where the deeper mind begins to listen. Here, new pathways form with ease. The effort dissolves, and transformation becomes something that happens naturally - from within, not through force.

Most of us know of hypnosis as a tool to stop smoking. Hypnosis works by changing the way the mind sees cigarettes. It breaks the link between daily triggers, like stress or routine, and the urge to smoke. At the same time, it builds a new self-image as someone free and healthy. Instead of relying on willpower alone, hypnosis makes quitting feel more natural by shifting habits at a deeper, subconscious level.

Similarly, hypnosis supports weight loss by gently shifting the habits and thought patterns that often get in the way. It helps the mind let go of old associations with food, like using it for comfort or reward, and replaces them with healthier responses.

Over time, the body begins to follow the mind's lead, making it easier to eat in a balanced way, feel satisfied, and stay consistent without relying on willpower alone.

The hypnotist has a good chance of helping someone eliminate habits that do not serve them; however, the person must be committed to making that change in their life.

Think of hypnosis as an efficient method similar to deep meditation. The approach focuses on removing the cravings, which can help you navigate more easily in the mindful choices of eating patterns. It is also a way to visualize a carefree and lighter version of yourself. This is important because for lasting change, you need to identify with another version of yourself.

Self-hypnosis can be an efficient and accessible tool to support you in becoming lighter. I have made a recording especially for this book, so you can try it out if you are curious. You simply listen to the sound file once a day when you go to bed. It is a pleasant guided meditation that is specially designed to get you into a deep trance, called the theta-state.

Trance sounds so new-age, but it is nothing new. We naturally go in and out of hypnosis during the day - for instance, when we drive long distances or before we fall asleep.

I use different techniques, like a visualization where you can identify with a lighter version of yourself. It takes about 20 minutes, and if you fall asleep while listening, it is just as efficient. It might even help you sleep at night if you have a hard time falling asleep. After just a week of listening to the recording, you will start feeling a difference in your daily behavior, and your cravings will lessen naturally.

This MP3 was created with your journey in mind - a companion to help you feel supported along the way. You can listen to the free recording at www.beforeshewastamed.com/free

If you ever feel curious to explore other themes - like awakening your energy, igniting your metabolism, or releasing habits that no longer serve you - you can find a small collection at www.beforeshewastamed.com/collection. Each audio is crafted to accompany you on your path toward more Quiet Power and Luxury.

Do you have any experience with meditation? Mindfulness? Hypnosis?

Would you like to give hypnosis a try? If yes, can you listen to a guided hypnosis before you go to sleep at night?

For me, it has turned out to be the most effective thing against cravings, but you wanna hear the crazy thing about it; I now started missing the cravings. It was somewhere I could put my mind and find temporary stress release.

The other day, I went into my good old comforting habit and pulled out a pint of Ben & Jerry's Caramel Dream. To my disappointment, the calming enjoyment did not come. Halfway through the pint and still nothing. I was baffled. I still devoured the whole thing but felt no joy.

I should congratulate myself - I had efficiently cured myself from that habit, but what followed was a surprising and deep feeling of loss. This used to be a place I could go for emotional comfort.

So, how do I release that combination of rewarding hormones in my brain in other ways?

If we aim to have a positive relationship with eating and drinking, it is important that we do not feel that we are missing out on the good life, because then it is a matter of time before we are back in our old habits. Not having these cravings frees up space and a feeling of freedom, but habits are strong. Hypnosis cannot stand alone.

The secret to being lighter is to focus on the small luxuries of your day. The more you deny yourself, the more you will crave it. The aim is to reach an everyday that gives you pleasure without making you fat. The important goal here is to reach a feeling of joy and ease with your food. Easier said than done, I know.

Allow me to step into my nutritionist shoes shortly to get the facts straight.

A lot of people focus on food and exercise - in other words, energy in and energy out. The problem with this is that the body is an amazing and very complicated system controlled by hormones, microtransmitters, and so on. When we try to simplify it, by, for instance, thinking in calories, we don't use the right tools to find weight balance.

When I studied Human Nutrition in Copenhagen in the 00s, we were taught to promote low-calorie foods so people could eat more without gaining weight. It was a one-size-fits-all model rooted in 90s thinking: carbs were fine, fat was not.

Clients logged their meals and wore exercise trackers, but we were told they likely underreported intake, essentially lying to us and themselves. Looking back, that approach was overly simplistic. The human body is far more complex, and metabolism varies widely.

To illustrate how misguided our standard understanding can be, consider this: Calories are measured by burning a food item in a clinical chamber and measuring the energy outcome. Needless to say that that is not how it works in the body.

This reductionist view completely overlooks the nuanced, hormone-driven complexity we've just explored through hypnosis and subconscious work. Relying too much on this info is like using a spoon when you need a knife. It is inefficient.

What if, instead, we saw the body as a dynamic energy system supported by tools like self-hypnosis, mindful eating, and emotional regulation? This way we can lessen cravings, stabilize energy doing the day, and boost our metabolism and digestion.

So let me ask you - when do you feel good in your skin?

Do you like your female curves?

How would you like your everyday habits to look when focusing on Quiet Luxury?

How often would you like to enjoy sweet or savory snacks?

How much exercise do you want to be part of your day?

How often would you like to enjoy a glass of wine, alcohol, or sugary drinks?

How often would you like to enjoy vegetables in your meals?

How often would you like to eat junk food?

What is a realistic weight balance for you based on your answers?

You can claim all the small enjoyments of life by finding a balance unique to you.

This can often be solved by changing habits gradually and focusing on mindful eating. If you feel good in a curvy version of yourself, you can still have optimal health. A good example of this is the Mediterranean Diet. This lifestyle is more calorie-dense but at the same time rich in healthy natural foods like unsaturated fats, like olives, olive oil, fatty fish, and nuts. Women in this part of the world are healthy, but curvier.

A woman's body is her own. No male-dominated industry has the right to dictate a woman's body, her desires, or her self-worth. And equally, we as women must stop measuring each other against outdated norms designed to keep us small - physically and metaphorically. Let's uplift one another and refuse to play by rules we never agreed to in the first place. Let us be kind to ourselves and our sisters. Let us take back our Quiet Power.

Our society has changed a lot within a short period. Physically hard labour no longer exists for most of us. Instead, we spend a lot of time at our desks or lounging in front of a screen. This means that we, in effect, need less energy and more nutrient-dense foods.

Intermittent fasting can be the lifestyle element that solves this. For most people, intermittent fasting will allow them to eat more of their favorite foods and thereby feel content. The most sustainable method is the 16:8. You fast for 16 hours and eat within an 8-hour window. This is doable for most people and will still maintain your muscle mass and metabolism. If this is too ambitious for you, you can do the 14:10 method with a 10-hour window of eating.

Could intermittent fasting fit your lifestyle of choice?

If yes, which model will work for you?

What is the first step you can take to start this new habit?

Do you need to include members of your household?

Feel free to share any extra reflections that come to mind here:

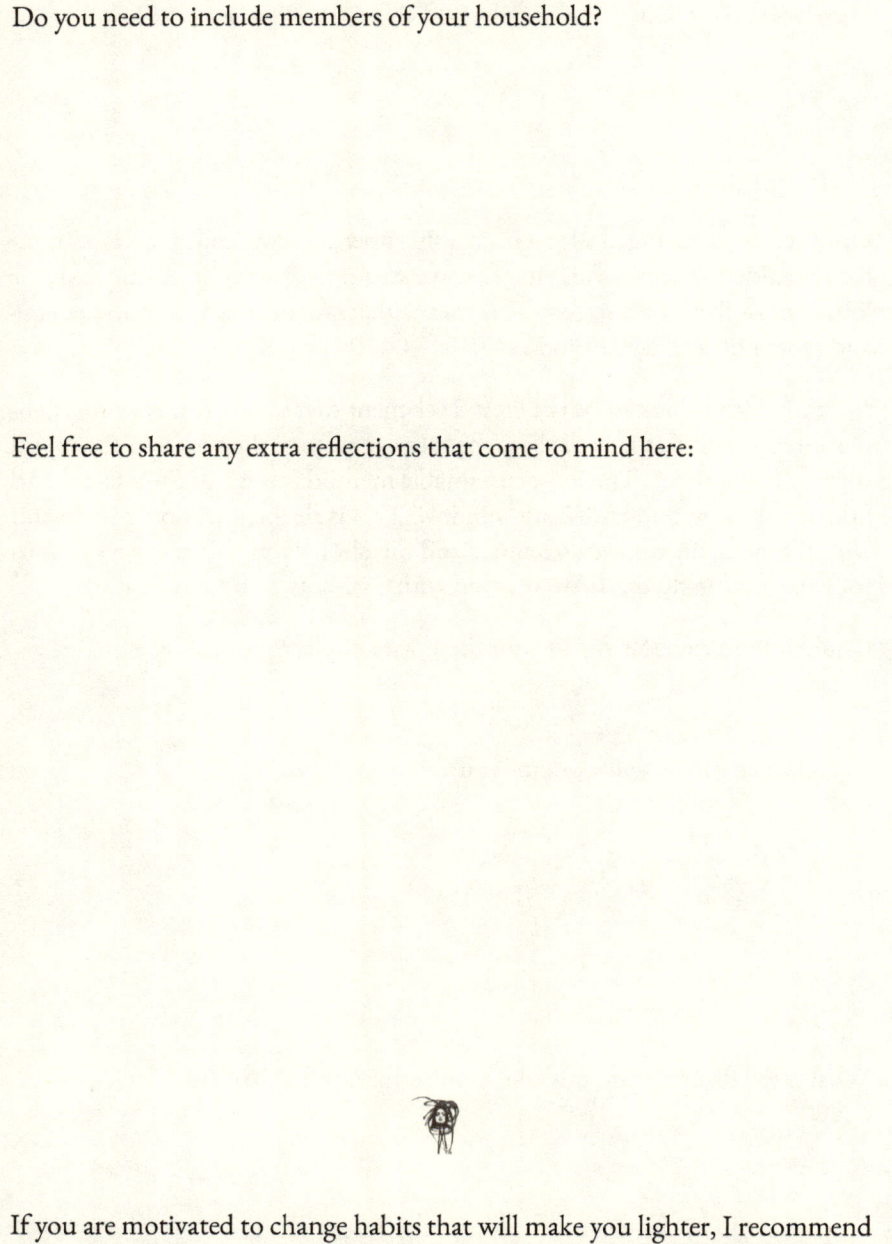

If you are motivated to change habits that will make you lighter, I recommend that you start by prioritizing the hypnosis recording. Then you can gradually change your habits, and I promise you that it is a different and easier task.

Choose a small task at a time and remember to reward yourself to get that feeling of Quiet Luxury. Whatever you do, do not choose any more diet plans, and please have a critical attitude towards so-called experts on social media. If in doubt, have your ChatGPT do a critical search on a new trend.

Right now, hot water with lemon and Himalayan salt is trending all over social media. Even famous women are swearing by it, as if a squeeze of lemon and a sprinkle of pink salt were a miracle cure.

But here's the truth: your body already detoxes itself through the liver and kidneys - it doesn't need help from a salted lemonade. Yes, lemon gives you some vitamin C, but beyond that, it won't burn fat, boost your metabolism, or reset your system. And too much salt can even put strain on your body. At best, it's a fancy placebo; at worst, it's a recipe for disappointment.

Quiet Luxury living is also to substitute with non-calorie options like good music, dancing, walking, drinking tea, and so on. Give it time to become a natural part of your system and your habits. You know that you have changed when you no longer enjoy your favorite cravings. But whatever you do, please don't make enemies of quality, nutritious foods.

If you are looking for deeper support, I offer a gentle masterclass to guide you further: www.beforeshewastamed.com/masterclass

For decades, the fashion industry, largely driven by male-dominated board-rooms, has robbed women of the joy of owning their soft curves and natural beauty. It's time to take that Quiet Power back, not just for ourselves but for every woman who has ever felt 'less than' because of a number on a scale, or a tag in a dress.

When you have a foundation of basic healthy habits, you will radiate health. Let us put one thing straight: you are a beautiful and unique woman, no matter your size.

Hypnosis, mindful eating, and semi-fasting became my path to balance. Tai Chi helps me regulate energy, but none of this would work if I were still chasing a model-thin ideal. I chose a different standard - my own. That choice made all the difference. Make sure yours is truly yours. Let peace of mind and a healthy, happy body be your quiet revolution. Be lighter!

How many frustrations and negative emotions can you save here?

If you have quality snacks at home, you save time and money dropping by the convenience store. If you spend 15 minutes a day, that is 7.6 hours a month (91 hours a year). An average buy of $5 a day is $152 a month ($1825 a year). Only adding empty calories.

List the ways you might save time and money:

How much time can you save yearly? _____ hours

How much money can you save yearly? $ _____

Your ChatGPT assistant suggests creating a Body-Love Playlist: "Let me build a Spotify playlist that celebrates your curves, softness, wildness, and joy." Think Pink meets PJ Harvey with some French café and soft tribal drums. You can dance instead of snacking.

Another beautiful way to feel lighter in both mind and body is through biking.

Consider biking

cykling

Imagine a gray Winter day in downtown Copenhagen. There is frost in the air, and there is a cold breeze coming from the ocean near us. It is early Saturday evening, and the sun seems to have never come out before it went down again.

Having a G&T in the cozy bar at the Tivoli hotel, I am enjoying the warmth and *hyggelige* atmosphere with a view of the street through a large panorama window.

The gentleman next to me is chatty and tells me that he is from Phoenix, Arizona. He is in Copenhagen for business and waiting for his colleagues so they can go out for some new Nordic Food. I, on the other hand, am expecting three girlfriends. We are planning to have sushi at the top of the hotel building and craft cocktails at one of our favorite bars afterward.

While I am chatting to this guy, my first girlfriend, Mirjana, makes her appearance on her city bike, swinging elegantly off the bike and placing it in the bike parking right in front of the window. She waves at me, and I wave back with a big smile. I am excited to have time with her since she has been very busy lately. I notice that she is looking stunning in a thigh-length black dress with her woolen winter coat hanging loose over her shoulders.

Mirjana is another example of a beautiful, remarkable woman that I am proud to call my friend. When she became unexpectedly pregnant in her thirties, she moved to the countryside to be with her partner, a *Jyde*, as we call people from mainland Denmark, often with an unspoken hint of conservatism.

Unfortunately, he turned out to be exactly that. Isolated from her friends and family, caring for a newborn with a man who didn't truly understand her, Mirjana felt deeply out of place.

She gave it a year, and then she moved back to Copenhagen, where she had been wise enough to keep her apartment. He eventually chose to follow her, and together they found a new balance in the city.

Instead of shaping herself to him, she stood in her Quiet Power. She remained anchored in her values, clear on what she needed, and unwilling to abandon herself in the name of love. That's strength. That's the mark of a modern heroine.

Mirjana and I first met as colleagues, both of us single women in our early thirties at the time. There was something unspoken - an instinctual recognition of the wild, untamed woman in each other. That spark drew us together, the same way Merete, Majken, and I had connected when we were in our twenties.

We went dancing. We traveled. We dared. I will not reveal too much here, but let's just say we crossed a few boundaries and laughed harder than we had in years. Eventually, our lives shifted, as they do, into new relationships and new chapters - but I still carry that chapter of my life with me.

Most often, Mirjana is full of energy and joy, like in this moment. Right behind her, the two other women come into view on their colorful bikes. Both have big, anticipating smiles on their faces. Both in party dresses and high heels. Quickly parking their bikes, they lean over to lock them with practised moves.

The American guy looks shocked. I thought that he simply appreciated the vision of my beautiful girlfriends, but the first thing out of his mouth was a stunned "how? How on Earth can your friends look that put-together when they ride their bikes here? It is a very strange phenomenon - it even seems like it adds to their looks that they have pink cheeks from the cold, and they look so natural and energized".

I looked at him in surprise. We have biked everywhere since we were kids, not giving it a second thought. You can even wear high heels because you get around so easily on a bike.

"Even though it is not legal to drive drunk on your bike, the police do not pay that much attention to it", I explain to him. "This way, we have the freedom to drink and drive, so to speak. When we are ready to go home, we just grab our bikes and go. Saving money on a taxi or other transportation, we have more money for the fun stuff", I smile at him.

The girls reach us, already in deep conversation with each other, catching up on recent events. I introduce them to my new acquaintance, and when his colleagues arrive too, he points to the girls and explains how they magically appeared on their bikes.

Of course, the Americans have all noticed that there are bikes everywhere in the city and that it is very dangerous to step into the bike lanes because they can easily be mistaken for the walkway.

When I admit to them that I don't even have a driver's license because I spend the money going to Australia instead, they almost fall off the tall bar chairs. Living in any city in Denmark, you truly do not need a car. It is hard to find a parking space, and it is expensive. Especially when we were students and had a very limited economy, bikes were the way to go.

We entertain our bar friends a bit more with anecdotes on bike-related stories, like Merete's hen party, where we drove her around Copenhagen in a Christiania bike. This bike is a sturdy, three-wheeled cargo bicycle with a large wooden box mounted at the front, designed to carry children, groceries, or anything from dogs to furniture. It's a popular eco-friendly transport choice in Denmark.

Wishing them a good night, we all crowd into the elevator, the volume of our voices rising when all four of us eagerly share the latest events in our lives. So unlike the men in our lives, we naturally use our curiosity and empathy to build each other up.

I invite you to consider whether you could use a bike where you live. We recently moved to Albuquerque in New Mexico, and were surprised by how bike-friendly the city is. Trails are going almost everywhere, so whenever we can, we jump on the bikes. We ended up buying e-bikes to be able to travel longer distances, and that works well for our lifestyle.

I have to admit that my partner's motivation was mostly to be able to drink and drive, but now he enjoys the wind in his hair as much as me. He has also learned that there is a limit to how drunk you can get after a close encounter with a nopal after a very wet evening at a beer festival. He drove straight into the ditch.

I couldn't help smiling a little to myself when I was picking out cactus spines afterward. Danish humor is dark and dry.

If you live in a place where biking is an option, whether on a mountain bike, a city bike, or an e-bike, consider giving it a try. You can even rent or borrow one from a friend to see if it suits you or your family. The rewards are easy to feel: a sense of freedom, and the bonus of effortless exercise built into your day.

Can you bike where you live?

Would you like to bike?

Is it possible to travel the distance to cafes and bars on a bike?

How often will you bike?

What type of bike would be ideal for you?

What invisible luggage could you leave behind on a ride - stress, worry, or expectation? What would you carry home instead?

If more thoughts arise, you can note them here:

You can save on shared rides, gasoline, parking, and maybe even the gym. If your household can reduce two cars to just one by exchanging the second car for an e-bike, you will save thousands of dollars on general expenses for an extra car.

Let us imagine that you sell your car and instead use your bike for work five days a week, at a distance of 5 miles each way. By biking for an hour, you have already done your exercise for the day. You will be part of a movement for cleaner air, especially if you live in a city.

Note your potential time and money savings here:

How much money will you save in a year if you start biking? $ _____

How can ChatGPT assist you here? It can suggest a local bike-friendliness report: "I can research how bikeable her city is, including paths, traffic safety, and elevation".

After a day of wind in your hair and movement in your body, you might just drift into sleep with the ease of a carefree child.

Sleep

søvn

What is the secret to a good night's sleep?

True luxury is diving under the duvet when you are tired, right? The contrast of the cold air in your bedroom and the warm comfort under your thick, soft duvet. Ahhh.

If you have slept in a luxury hotel, you might have had an amazing sleep experience - the white, crisp, clean linen from high-count natural fibers. The bed hugs you just right. The beautiful decor lamps are on the bedside tables.

Visiting Las Vegas some years ago, we stayed at the Delano. The bed was enormous, and so was the bathroom. I almost didn't feel like leaving the room. I have never in my life felt that comfortable - now that is Quiet Luxury!

Since then, I have tried to replicate this feeling. Within our budget, we found beds with similar qualities. I buy high-thread-count organic cotton or linen fitted sheets and duvet covers.

Did you know that Danish parents leave their infants to sleep in a carriage outside so that the baby can sleep more deeply?

There was a news story in the US some years ago when a Danish couple was having coffee in a cafe in downtown New York. The carriage with their baby was left outside the window. Someone called the police on them, and it became a big thing, but really, it was just a culture clash.

In a household with three cats and two dogs, we sleep in one big pile at night. Our great Dane Freja takes up most of the space, so we sleep in a giant bed made up from two king-size mattresses put together on the floor.

I love the closeness and feeling of safety. Even though I often wake up with a lot of tension in my body because I can not stretch out my legs or even move. In contrast, I sometimes choose to sleep in the guest bedroom. Going to bed early with a good audiobook adds a bit of Quiet Luxury.

If anything has an impact on your day, it is how you sleep at night. Women often carry the invisible load of planning, caring, and worrying.

Those restless nights where you toss and turn, or you fall asleep and maybe wake up in the middle of the night. It will leave you exhausted the next day. It also has an effect on your hormones, which has a lot of negative side effects. It can weaken your immune system, as well as being a contributor to possible weight gain.

If this is an issue in your life, I am sure that you have already looked into what to do about it, so I am not gonna go into all the advice that's out there. Your ChatGPT can be of assistance here, too. The better it gets to know you, the more efficient advice it can give you.

I am going through a period right now where I fall asleep, but most nights, I wake up around 3 am and feel very much awake. The explanation seems to be perimenopause. It is very frustrating and leaves me exhausted. What works for me is getting out in the natural light early in the day - either doing my Tai Chi routine in the garden or going for a walk. This activates the natural melatonin levels at night.

Another efficient habit is using CBD/CBN, designed especially for sleep. I do a couple of drops half an hour before I want to sleep.

While this helps me fall asleep, it does not help me when I am wide awake in the middle of the night. The most efficient sleep formula is then listening to my hypnosis recording. I use the combined sleep and weight loss recording I mentioned in the chapter Be Lighter to reach my subconscious when drifting off.

Even though we focus mostly on our outer world in this book, I cannot emphasize enough that happiness and contentment come from within. The outer world is an expression of your inner world.

Eckhart Tolle is the author behind the bestseller The Power of Now. I cannot count how many times I have read that book. I keep learning more and more every time I read it again.

Tolle emphasizes that to calm our thoughts and stay in the now, we will avoid stress because stress is either focusing too much on the past or the future. You probably recognize the frustration when you are in bed and cannot help but stress about the next day's work or maybe how you are gonna make ends meet. In other words, you are caught up in the future - a future that doesn't exist.

The solution is to stay in the now, and it can be helpful to focus on something very pleasant and relaxing, like a hypnosis recording, to escape your mind and relax into your body.

For many women, reclaiming rest and reconnecting with their bodies in this way is not just calming, it is a quiet act of empowerment in a world that asks a lot of them.

Or perhaps in the spirit of being free and untamed, we can take inspiration from our Latina sisters, who remind us that embodiment can also mean going out, laughing, and losing ourselves in joy, rather than in restless thoughts.

If you have started listening to the free hypnosis MP3 when you go to bed, I hope that it has already helped you find a better sleep and weight balance. If not, you can download it at www.beforeshewastamed.com/free

What invisible weight do you sometimes carry into the night?

How can you lay it down before sleep, so your dreams can be lighter?

Which solutions work for you right now?

What does not work?

Imagine a period of your life where you woke each morning fully restored. What would shift in your body, your mood, your creativity, your relationships?

If worries keep you up, what can you do to take one step towards worry-free nights?

If you want to exchange sleeping tablets for more natural solutions, can you make a plan with your doctor?

The payoff to sleep through the night, every night, is priceless. The luxury of having energy to enjoy the day and radiate health. There is also money to save if you skip sleeping tablets. The cheapest sleep tablets on the American market come out to $816 a year ($68 a month), but can be much more if you use a name brand.

List your potential savings here:

How much money can you save yearly? $ _____

> How can your ChatGPT assistant help you get more rest?

Would you like to experience more nights wrapped in that luxurious feeling that comes with traveling?

Travel

rejse

Would you like to enjoy the ultimate luxury at a 5-star hotel? By saving on smaller things during your trip, you can upgrade to a better hotel.

When I was a student and flying from Budapest to Copenhagen, I did not realize that there were two airports, and I almost missed my flight because I ended up at the wrong airport. When I came storming in and the gate was about to close, a startled airline hostess dryly told me that the airplane was full.

For a moment, I thought it was too late, but then she smiled and told me that she would upgrade me to business class for free.

I was so stressed that the information simply did not compute. I realized that something was off when I got onto the plane, and a steward politely asked me if he could take my coat and put it on a hanger in a small locker. When I checked my boarding pass, I was surprised to see that I had a seat in the 2nd row and settled in on the wide, comfortable space.

Needless to say, I had way too much complimentary champagne on my way home. In Danish we say; "Heldet følger de skøre" (luck follows the mad). Or at least that is what my mom says.

Today, Fernando is my personal travel agent - and much more. He comes from a family of seasoned travelers, and together we share a deep love for exploration and discovery.

I feel truly fortunate to have found a partner who not only understands me but shares my hunger for adventure. With him, I have left the drama of past relationships behind and grown into a steadier, more grounded version of myself.

Moving to Mexico right after we married threw us into the deep end. Building a life and a business together forced us to really see each other, beyond the surface. Our cultural differences sometimes clashed, and the pressure nearly broke us in that first year. But instead of splitting, we bent and expanded the boundaries of our relationship. We made it work. Eight years in, we balance each other out.

You could say we are living a modern version of the American Dream. Not the picket-fence kind, but one defined by wide horizons and a sense of spaciousness that seems built into American culture. What fascinates me most is how that dream has evolved from ownership to experience. It is less about settling down and more about expanding what feels possible.

I think it's time we start speaking of the U.S. as we do of Europe – a patchwork of distinct regions, each with its own flavor and rhythm. Every state feels like a small country of its own, from the soulful South to the restless coasts and the vast, silent deserts. The U.S. is a living collage of climates, cuisines, and ways of seeing the world.

Between vibrant Mexico and the wide-open landscapes of the United States, I have discovered a quiet kind of freedom - one that isn't loud, but deeply felt. The freedom to reinvent myself, to belong nowhere and everywhere at once. Both Mexicans and Americans, in their own ways, strike me as openhearted, generous, and easygoing.

Because travel has taught us so much, I will share our hard-earned recipe for traveling smart:

When choosing your travels, let your values guide you. What exactly are you looking for? Relaxing at the beach, getting in shape in a Tai Chi or yoga boot camp on an exotic island, learning a new language, taking a spiritual journey, exploring a new city, or a new culture? Your imagination is the limit. How can you reclaim Quiet Luxury for yourself?

The key is to travel light. Skip the checked luggage and bring a medium-sized backpack; you will be surprised at how much it can hold. It fits under your seat, and unlike roller bags, it won't be taken from you if the flight is full. That way, you save precious time when you land.

On low-budget airlines, checked baggage fees can add up quickly, no matter where you are.

In the U.S., carriers like Spirit and Frontier typically charge around $35 to $50 for the first checked bag. In Europe, budget airlines such as Ryanair and easyJet charge between €25 and €70, depending on the route and when you book the bag.

In Mexico, low-cost carriers like Volaris and VivaAerobús can charge $50 or more for checked luggage. Across the board, these airlines keep base fares low by making luggage a major source of profit, so if you're traveling light, you win. If not, it adds up fast.

If you travel with family or friends, do not pay to choose your seats. Instead, take the opportunity to read a good book or watch your favorite show. Especially if you're usually the one doing all the packing and planning, this is your reminder that it's okay to carve out time for yourself. You've earned it. Turn it into a *hygge* moment, knowing that you will be saving money this way.

Or how about traveling solo - no compromises, returning to your untamed self?

In the U.S., carriers like Spirit and Frontier charge anywhere from $5 to $50, depending on location. In Europe, Ryanair and easyJet offer similar pricing, with fees ranging from €5 to €30.

Mexican budget airlines like Volaris and VivaAerobús also charge $5 to $30 for seat selection. It's a global pattern: the cheaper the base fare, the more you'll pay to sit where you want.

Do not buy food and drinks on the plane or at the airport. Save calories and money on low-quality, overpriced items. Bring your beautiful flask and tap water at the airport. This way, you can save at least $30 each way. Bring a sandwich or buy one in your local delicatessen before you head for the airport, or if it is a shorter trip, simply eat at home before you go.

If you consider check-in luggage and choosing your seat as a luxury, you might want to choose a higher-end airline. You can have your ChatGPT research for you.

But just consider this: If you are going on vacation with your partner, you can now upgrade to a four or five-star hotel or dinner at a gourmet restaurant because just by getting there, you saved at least $320 on your round trip. That means $640 in spending money if you are two.

If luxury were not about money but about freedom, presence, and discovery, what would your next trip look and feel like?

How often do you travel to see family or go on vacation?

How much can you save yearly if you bring food/snacks from home? Or eat at home? $ _____

How much will you save a year if you do not choose a seat? $ _____

If you travel light and don't check in luggage? $ _____

How much can you save on a trip all in all in a year? $ _____

How much time can you save in a year? _____ hours

If you are in the habit of buying souvenirs that end up breaking or collecting dust in your home, you might wanna skip that. If you see something you want, sleep on it if you can, or consider taking a photo instead for your memories. Either way, make sure that it is worth taking home. Only buy it if it truly has value for you. Imagine it in your home, will you use it?

If you are considering visiting multiple countries in Europe, buy individual tickets from low-budget companies. It is cheaper to fly in Europe because of the competition.

As a rule of thumb, Northern Europe is colder and more expensive than countries in Eastern and Southern Europe. All countries have something unique to offer, so make sure that you take your time.

For the ultimate luxury experience, you might consider going on a cruise. The reputation as being very expensive is not justified, especially since the hotel and restaurant prices have gone up significantly lately.

Make sure to pick a cruise line that has smaller ships and better amenities for that luxury feeling. You want quality meals, drinks, and service. We always buy our selected cruise when there is a sale, and then we sit down and choose the one we are most excited about at that time.

I am not sure if it is because of my Viking inheritance, but I love being on the ocean.

On our last cruise to the Caribbean Islands, they offered Tai Chi at sunrise - it was a beautiful experience to see the sun rising while looking over the vast ocean, taking in the sun's energy. I even go to the gym on cruises because I can look out at the front of the ship while exercising, and it makes me feel good before indulging in gourmet food and good wine.

Dinner every night is a delight. I love dressing up for a 3-course gourmet experience - wearing my silk dresses, trying out different hairstyles, and statement earrings. I make sure to make the most of my tan with light gold makeup.

After dinner, we walk around and around the ship, enjoying the sundown before we go for live music. On occasion, a whale or dolphin will add even more wonder to our experience.

Could a cruise vacation be something for you? What part of the world would you go to if you could choose any destination?

What would make it feel like the ultimate luxury vacation?

What invisible luggage do you tend to pack with you - stress, guilt, expectations - and what would it feel like to leave it behind?

On a smaller scale, a day trip can have a similar effect. If you could go for a day trip or weekend trip, where would you go?

Additional reflections:

If you want to stretch your travel budget even further, especially with hotel prices soaring, consider using a travel-focused credit card. These can unlock savings, upgrades, and perks that make a big difference.

Note your potential time and money savings here:

How much can you save all together in a year? $ _____

How much time can you save all together in a year? _____ hours

Your ChatGPT can be of tremendous help here. Ask it what tools it has access to to plan your dream vacation, or even better, tell it to teach your partner to be your personal travel agent. That is what I did, and he comes up with brilliant suggestions these days.

Finances

økonomi

As I am writing this book, something tragic happened - there was a severe fire in our taproom in Tijuana.

Imagine the shock of receiving a call from the neighbors, only to then see a clip on the local news of firefighters battling the blaze, surrounded by thick clouds of smoke. It was honestly very surreal. We had put our heart and soul into that place and had rented it out when we left TJ a bit more than a year ago.

Luckily, everyone was evacuated safely, and the fire was put out before it reached the back part, where the brewery and kitchen are. Apparently, a worker welding next door had not noticed that a spark flew and landed between the wall, where it slowly ignited and eventually turned into a full-on fire.

Suddenly, worry clouded our lives again.

We risked losing our rental income overnight, with no real insurance options available in Mexico. And, of course, it all happened while we were already facing extra expenses, like costly car repairs. None of it was planned or budgeted for. On top of the financial strain came the natural worries - the kind that steal your sleep and quietly erode the quality of daily life.

We went for a long walk in the fall sunshine and made a plan. We decided to cut down on some of the nice-to-have activities in our lives. Some of the luxuries.

First, we canceled that gourmet dinner we had planned at our favorite restaurant, Farm To Table. Fernando gave up on getting more mezcal, the dogs would have to go back to kibble for a while, and I would postpone my hairdresser appointment another month.

More cooking at home and eating out at more casual spots, and we could take money out of our savings to get the bar repaired and reestablish our rental income. Then we biked to the local brewery and drank away our sorrows.

Later that day, our former employees called us from the blackened taproom to let us know they were there for us. They send us videos with shovels in hand, and the slow progress of getting rid of the wet debris. It wasn't until then that I shed a tear. It was very moving that they were there for us like that.

Then my *cuñado* Franco stepped in to save the day. He told us the family would cover the repair costs and even restore our monthly rental income, knowing how much we needed it to cover the green card expenses.

If you're not already familiar with how tightly knit Mexican families can be, this is a perfect example. What a relief it was. As I write this, just days after the accident, the rebuilding has already begun, with my brother-in-law taking charge of the project.

Part of this tale is that we took over the space in 2018 and did a total renovation. We ended up extending the back part in 2019 to turn it into a brewery. We invested a large amount of money, and then COVID happened, and we had to close down for a year.

When we closed down for good in 2023, we had not earned much on the project, but at least we had supported four employees and even put our youngest employee through physiotherapy school. When we rented it out, we calculated that it would take a bit more than four years to earn back the investment.

No matter your budget, you will need a buffer in your account to be worry-free in your life. Shit happens, and you cannot always control it. Nothing makes you feel more tamed by life than strained finances.

I grew up in a family where my father's company earned a solid amount of money until it didn't. My father, coming from a very poor upbringing on a farm with six siblings, wanted more from life. He quickly developed a liking for the "loud luxuries".

When I was six, we moved to a spacious, newly built house, and my sister Ann and I no longer had to share a room. I still remember the excitement when I chose my room that smelled like fresh paint.

High-tech items from Bang & Olufsen moved in with us. After that came a collection of good wine and a car for each of my parents, with a mobile phone in the main car - it was the size of a brick back then in the 1980s.

When my father's company didn't do so well anymore, he started gambling more. For years, he hid the fact that money was getting scarcer. When we became teenagers, he finally turned himself in for skimming off money and not being able to pay taxes.

I still remember the day it happened and the relief in his eyes. He went to jail for a while, and with that, there was absolutely no money. He had even spent our child's savings.

From one day to the next, I had to figure out what money was worth since I could no longer go to my dad when I wanted a new pair of jeans or fun money to spend with my friends. I escaped to Australia by getting a loan from my bank. I told them it was for a driver's license since it was hard to get a loan at the age of 17. More about this life-changing journey later.

Weeks later in Sydney, a bank machine swallowed my credit card, and the stern-faced teller cut it in half before a long line of onlookers. I burned with humiliation. Unlike the safety net of my now Mexican family, I had no one to turn to - and truthfully, I had put myself in that position.

Back in Denmark, I couldn't even afford a night out with friends. But it was part of growing up, part of learning that I had to take care of myself. My baseline had shifted for good after my father's bankruptcy. Since then, I've always kept a small savings set aside for life's inevitable mood swings.

If your life choices have placed the power of your finances in someone else's hands, it's time to take that power back.

As a homemaker, never forget that your work carries equal weight to your partner's - it is the foundation that allows everything else to function. And if you've pressed pause on your career or chosen part-time work while caring for young children, you are not "less", but the system often undervalues you.

Missed raises, smaller pensions, lost opportunities: these are the invisible costs. In a divorce, they can become dangerous vulnerabilities. I have seen it too many times.

Stepping into your Quiet Power might mean sitting down with your partner and creating a plan that honors both of you. Building a family is not a woman's burden - it is shared work, shared love, and shared responsibility. A partnership rooted in equality doesn't just protect you; it elevates you both.

It reminds me of the lyrics of Paris Paloma's song Labour:

> "... all day, every day, therapist, mother, maid,
> nymph, then a virgin, nurse, then a servant.
> Just an appendage, live to attend him
> so that he never lifts a finger
> 24/7 baby machine
> so he can live out his picket-fence dreams...."
>
> Paris Paloma

Watching the inspiring video from one of her live concerts, I agree with Paris's statement: "Our voices are so powerful together". The cacophony feels like a shift in our time that I hope this book can support. It is time to reclaim our Quiet Power and support each other.

To grow into a magnificent white swan and leave our younger, grey selves behind, we must do exactly that - stand in our Quiet Power. Gathering every scattered fragment into the woman we were always meant to be.

This wholeness includes our sexuality. We are cyclical beings - passionate, intuitive, and wild by design. It is not something to be managed or silenced. Never let a man tame that rhythm. If love begins to fragment you, if he cannot meet your depth or honor your truth, walk away. Let his wounds remain his own, do not carry them as yours.

Your body was created for pleasure, for connection, for energy that nourishes rather than drains. If he cannot bring you to ecstasy, guide him, but never bend yourself into smaller shapes for his comfort. He was drawn to your untamed essence in the first place. Do not let him teach you how to dim it.

Now back to the less interesting, but unfortunately necessary, foundations of our modern lives. I am not claiming to know much about how to deal with finances in different parts of the world. Building on the principles displayed here, I will just make a few points:

You need less insurance if you have fewer things.

You can keep your health insurance at a minimum when you are healthier.

A habit of saving on water, electricity, and gas in small amounts. Turn off lights when you are not in the room, and keep the room temperature in your home at a pleasant temperature, but not overly cool or hot.

In the US, the Department of Energy estimates that you can save 10% annually by setting your temperature back by 10 degrees Fahrenheit during 8-hour periods regularly. For instance, when the house is unoccupied during the day, or if you want a cooler night temperature. You can find more saving tips online or ask ChatGPT.

Keeping a wilder garden with native plants will need less watering, which will have an impact on your finances as well as the environment. If we stop using unnecessary chemicals, butterflies and bees will come back in numbers. You might also wanna consider solar power as an option to minimize your electricity bills.

Keep a close eye on which subscriptions you actually use and cancel the rest.

In our home, we switch between Netflix, Apple TV, and Paramount these days. We explore one provider and then cancel the others until we don't think there is more to see, and then we switch again. If you cancel one subscription at $21 a month, you can save $252 a year.

I recently started listening to podcasts as well, and can find a lot of inspiration on selected apps. One very important thing about this is to avoid commercials. Not only are they stealing away your precious time, but they are also influencing your choices of buying things by clever manipulation. If you have fewer subscriptions, you can choose Premium versions, commercial-free, and still save money.

Quiet Luxury, am I right?

Is your Dropbox, iCloud, or Drive full and asking you to buy extra space? You might wanna have a look at what you are storing. Is it time for a clean-up? It is the same principle as when things in your home start piling up. You can save at least $10 a month ($120 a year) if you don't pay for storage.

In short, keep an awareness of which basics are in line with your values and which ones you can live without. Do not upgrade your electronics like mobiles, TVs, and so on until they die. When you save money on basic invisible expenses, you will have more money for the fun stuff.

If you peeled back the noise of subscriptions, upgrades, and consumer pressure, what would true financial Quiet Luxury look like for you?

List all of your subscriptions here:

-
-
-
-
-
-
-
-

Do you currently have subscriptions for something you rarely use?

Can you get more out of your subscriptions?

Is your internet provider the best and cheapest in your area?

Can you change to a more affordable mobile subscription?

Does your insurance cover your basics, or can you change it for a better one?

Do you have health insurance that fits your needs?

Does your bank offer the best interest rate, or is it time to change to another?

Can you put your savings in a high-yield account?

List the ways you might save time and money:

How much money can you save in a year? $ _____

If you allow commercials to take up 15 minutes on average a day, it will steal 7 hours a month or 84 hours a year of your precious time. Time that you could have spent on something rewarding, something adding to Quiet Luxury living.

How much time can you save in a year? _____ hours

You can roleplay with your ChatGPT assistant: "You are my financial advisor. What advice do you have for me currently, based on my financial habits..." and "surprise me with an option I never would have come up with myself".

Additional reflections:

As a woman, what invisible costs - in time, energy, or freedom - are you still paying, and what would it mean to release them?

Clothes

tøj

If you look at pictures from your life and you have a similar style in most of them, maybe it is time to try something new?

On the other hand, if you feel that your current style truly reflects who you are, you can save time and money by doing nothing at all. Both ways, you stand in your Quiet Power.

If you do feel like it is time for a change, I would like you to remember when you were a kid and played dress up with your mom's clothes and shoes. This is the carefree, creative spirit you wanna bring back to life.

Now that you are saving time and money, you most likely have the energy to be a bit more creative with your daily choices.

First of all, I suggest that you reorganize your wardrobe. I highly recommend hanging up most of your clothes on hangers. Imagine that your wardrobe is a mini clothes store.

It can be as simple as hanging a rod from the ceiling or wall if you don't have space for a walk-in closet. I promise it will be worth it. Clothes quickly become a mess when put on shelves. You need the overview to choose different combinations on an everyday basis, where a lot is going on.

Can this be a solution for you?

If yes, where in your home will you build this?

Can you do it yourself, or do you need help?

Quality lasts forever - will you believe me if I tell you that I have items that are easily 25 years old?

I don't buy clothes for months, but focus instead on combining my existing clothes in different ways. When I buy something, I have had my eyes on it for a while. My last buy was a beautiful dark-green silk kimono from Kim & Ono.

When I visit Copenhagen, I have access to an outlet sale with beautiful designer clothes. I save up to go there once a year and pick out just one item that makes me feel like a model.

Why not plan a glamorous midweek day now and then? Treat yourself by spending some of your saved money on dinner at a favorite café or restaurant with a partner or friend - and dress for the occasion. I am all for comfort, but that doesn't mean style has to be monotonous. This is where contrast living comes in.

Since I spend most of my time working from home, there are days I barely step out of my *hyggebukser* (pyjamas). All the more reason it feels uplifting to dress up a little when I do go out. It only takes five minutes to choose something different from the wardrobe, yet it shifts the whole mood.

I often get compliments from other women when I wear my pink maxi dress, which is so comfortable but also makes me feel a bit glamorous. If you admire something about a woman in passing, please compliment her and put a smile on her face. We all know that there are days we need it.

Quiet Luxury, as a fashion statement, was born in Europe in the 18th century and had a revival in 2023 when more flashy brands were replaced with understated quality.

A perfect example is the Danish shoe brand Ecco. All of a sudden, it became popular worldwide because it hit the mark of casual quality.

Whether you are into fashion or not, you can enjoy wearing clothes made from natural fibres like organic cotton or silk. It is a bit like the way you style your home. Using a neutral palette, you can use an accent color to set off your style. For instance, with a beautiful silk scarf or a pair of classy high-heeled shoes.

Our choice of clothes can also be an act of Quiet Power.

In the 1970s in Scandinavia, many women quietly stopped wearing bras - not as a loud protest, but as a calm refusal to be shaped by someone else's expectations. There were no speeches, no banners - just a quiet choice made every morning in front of the mirror.

This kind of power doesn't shout; it simply is. It reminds us that true rebellion doesn't always need noise - sometimes, the softest acts carry the deepest change.

In a world still full of pressure to conform, this Quiet Power invites us to listen inward, to choose comfort over performance, and to let our choices speak for us without apology.

You might recall that my midlife crisis began after those bike accidents in Copenhagen. As everything in my life started to shift, so did my sense of style. I wanted to dress in a way that reflected the woman I was becoming. So I signed up for a seminar with stylist Tobi Wiberg from my network, women-in-business.

Through her easy guidance, I discovered the quiet magic of accessories. A simple scarf or a pair of well-chosen earrings can completely transform a look - and help you make the most of what you already have. With this approach, you need fewer pieces in your wardrobe, which means less decision fatigue, less spending, and more ease.

For eight weeks, she challenged ten women through fun exercises to make full use of their wardrobes and only supplied them with a few accessories to make it more interesting. It was so much fun, and we bonded over our different body shapes and new style choices. It felt good to reclaim time to spoil myself and share the change with other women.

You can invite some of the women in your life over to make a Pinterest moodboard if you feel like taking that extra step towards your style of choice.

Getting into the creative zone and having fun can be a good excuse for a girls' night. It is a great inspiration and it can save you a lot of buys that end up at the bottom of your closet. You can even exchange items as part of the fun. That item that never really suited you might look just right on your girlfriend.

Would you like to invite a group of women over to create moodboards and perhaps engage in some networking?

If yes, who will you invite and why?

In detail, how will you make this happen?

If your wardrobe were a mirror of your values, what truth would it reflect back to you today?

When has clothing made you feel untamed - not dressing for anyone else, but purely for your own joy and freedom?

Do you admire a style and would like to try it out?

If something comes to mind, you can find some pictures online and use those images to picture-search for similar items and copy that look.

Looking back at my mood board from that time, I can see how clearly my values around freedom were expressed. I have always loved natural fibers paired with a touch of lace. Choosing comfort in clothing doesn't have to mean choosing dullness.

In fact, isn't it wonderful that we get to dress up every day, with the freedom to wear whatever we like? Not all women have that privilege. Many still live within rigid, male-dominated cultures that restrict even this simple expression - trying to tame her spirit.

If you buy a piece of clothing once a month on average at $30 ($360 a year) but exchange that habit for quality, you can buy an exclusive piece once a year instead. Since that will probably last you a lifetime, you will save money in the long run and feel like a million. Less is more.

If you buy a fashion magazine every month and instead use the free online inspiration, you can save $6 a month ($72 a year). In the same way commercials have a strong influence on your consumer habits, not exposing yourself to the temptations of magazines will save you a lot of money. You will need fewer items because it has a timeless appeal.

Would you like to explore the apps you already have for fashion inspiration? Simply have your ChatGPT do the research.

If you haven't used some clothing items in a year, sell them off or give them to charity. If you buy investment pieces, you can sell them again. Let us make a sustainable trend this way. If you choose organic, sustainable items not made from child labour, together we can make a change.

Reflect on where time and money could be freed:

How much money can you save a year? $ _____

How much time can you save a year? _____ hours

How can your ChatGPT assistant support you fashion-wise? Would you like it to turn into your personal fashion advisor?

Networking

netværk

This is where women excel. We are much better at networking than men.

When it comes to feeling luxurious, nothing makes you feel good and safe like friendship. True friends cannot be bought and are worth more than things you can buy with money.

My close friends all have one thing in common - they are curious, open-minded, and they really listen. They don't just wait for their turn to speak. Every time I see them, I am surprised by how we instantly reconnect, as if time has not passed at all. When I learned Motivational Interviewing (MI) through work, it came naturally to me because it is part of our culture.

I cannot write this chapter without honoring my friend Carina. She is, quite simply, Miss Network. We first met on a rainy day in Copenhagen, when she picked me up for my very first WIB meeting, and from that moment, we were instant friends.

Carina has stretched my comfort zone by inviting me to speak at one of her conferences. Her colorful, chatty energy is a vibrant contrast to my calm, quiet nature. Together, we hosted countless WIB events over the years, supporting each other both personally and professionally. Through her books and speeches, she has inspired thousands. If anyone embodies Quiet Power, it is her.

Leaving my friends behind in Copenhagen is, without a doubt, the steepest price I have paid for moving abroad.

If you're wondering, how many brilliant women can she possibly have in her life? I promise, I am not exaggerating. But I am not speaking of brilliance in the loud, self-promoting sense. I am speaking of women whose power hums quietly beneath the surface – women who have known pain, who have rebuilt themselves, who lead not with noise but with presence.

As I wrote in the introduction, many of us learn to dim our light for a time - sometimes out of fear, sometimes out of love, sometimes simply to survive. Yet there's a moment, often unexpected, when another woman sees us clearly and reminds us who we are. That's where quiet power is born, not from independence alone.

I have learned my own strength through those cycles of dimming and remembering. Later, I will tell you about a time when I lost myself and how I found my way back.

In Mexico, I had to learn Spanish, and I was excited about expanding my skill set by adding another language. I thought I would learn fast, but that was not the case. It was not from lack of trying. I found a Spanish teacher and went twice a week. I simultaneously used a professional app, Synergy Spanish, and I prioritized practising Spanish every day.

After a year, my Spanish was okay but not great. After another year, it had not improved that much, and after that, it just started being embarrassing when I quickly hit a wall in everyday conversations. To make matters worse, some of our employees had very limited English skills, so I needed to communicate fluently in Spanish.

There is a meme where a Latina barista at a coffee shop takes orders from customers who believe that their Spanish skills are much better than they think. She asks a customer some questions about their coffee preferences, and the customer answers "*sí*" to all of them. The barista then lines up several different coffees on the counter. The customer asks which one is hers, and the barista dryly replies "*sí*," and turns away.

Just writing this, I feel embarrassed. It hits too close to home. That is me right there. Okay, granted, my Spanish is at least good enough to handle ordering a coffee, but still. Most of the time, I am too proud to simply say when I do not understand.

Someone said that to be able to learn something new, you have to be willing to be bad at it first. It made me realize that pride might be my greatest obstacle to truly learning Spanish.

Finally accepting this, I had to decide to simply give up or put in some more work. I have started using my app again on my daily walks, just 10 minutes a day. In addition, I am meeting up with a language group once a week. Slowly, I am starting to speak more fluently.

In Tijuana, however, it was lonely to be excluded from many conversations. It was hard to find other female friends with shared values.

I had lots of acquaintances through Fernando's friends and the bar environment, but I missed connecting with women who really got me. Eventually, though, I did resonate with women who became good, trusted friends, and that sisterhood made a difference in my new life. I still carry that untamed Latina spirit with me.

Now that I have moved to the US, I make sure to prioritize networking. After almost two years here, I occasionally enjoy the company of some amazing women whom I have met through different networks.

I took a class in hypnosis as part of a more holistic lifestyle. That led to an enlightening seminar in Sedona, where I met this amazing woman, Nikiya, from New York. We bonded over cocktails and found out that we have a lot in common, including a rebel streak.

Nikiya is a vibrant, outgoing Black woman with striking blond extensions and a presence you don't forget. When she was young, she had the misfortune to fall in love with a guy who turned out to be violent and manipulative. Despite this, she got herself an education and a career while bringing up two small children, with support from her equally strong mother.

When her kids were old enough, she took a leap most people only dream of - she left a well-paid job and moved to Florida to follow a spiritual calling and build a life on her terms. It takes immense courage to do what she did. She chose herself, not out of selfishness, but out of wisdom. She put on her oxygen mask first, as every woman should.

Later, while exploring Albuquerque, I went to a traditional Temazcal lodge and met Elizabeth, who had just moved here from Denver. She is a kind, intelligent, dark-haired Persian-American woman who had fallen in love and was brave enough to start her life over to be with him.

Like Nikiya, she left a stable career, in her case, as a biomedical lab technician, to follow a more spiritual path and become an entrepreneur. I sense a depth and strength in her that comes from losing her former partner to suicide. We have all been shaped by life in different ways, and by sharing it, we all become more resilient.

Life has a way of supporting you when you step outside your comfort zone. Elizabeth and I quickly discovered how much we have in common, and now we explore new corners of the city together, cheering each other on in life and business. She was also the one who first introduced me to the wonders of ChatGPT.

So my questions for you are:

Do you prioritize your friends?

Or have you outgrown friendships and would like to find new ones?

If we go one step further, would you like to learn a new language or a new craft?

Are you ready to change jobs and need better skills?

Let us work on adding more moments of Quiet Luxury to your life.

Brainstorm your interests and make a list:

-
-
-
-
-

Choose one that excites you the most right now:

How can you implement a new interest into your life? Describe it in detail:

Whatever your choice, be realistic and consider whether the everyday work you have to put into it is doable. Do not start until you have considered if you have the energy to follow through - you have to enjoy the journey.

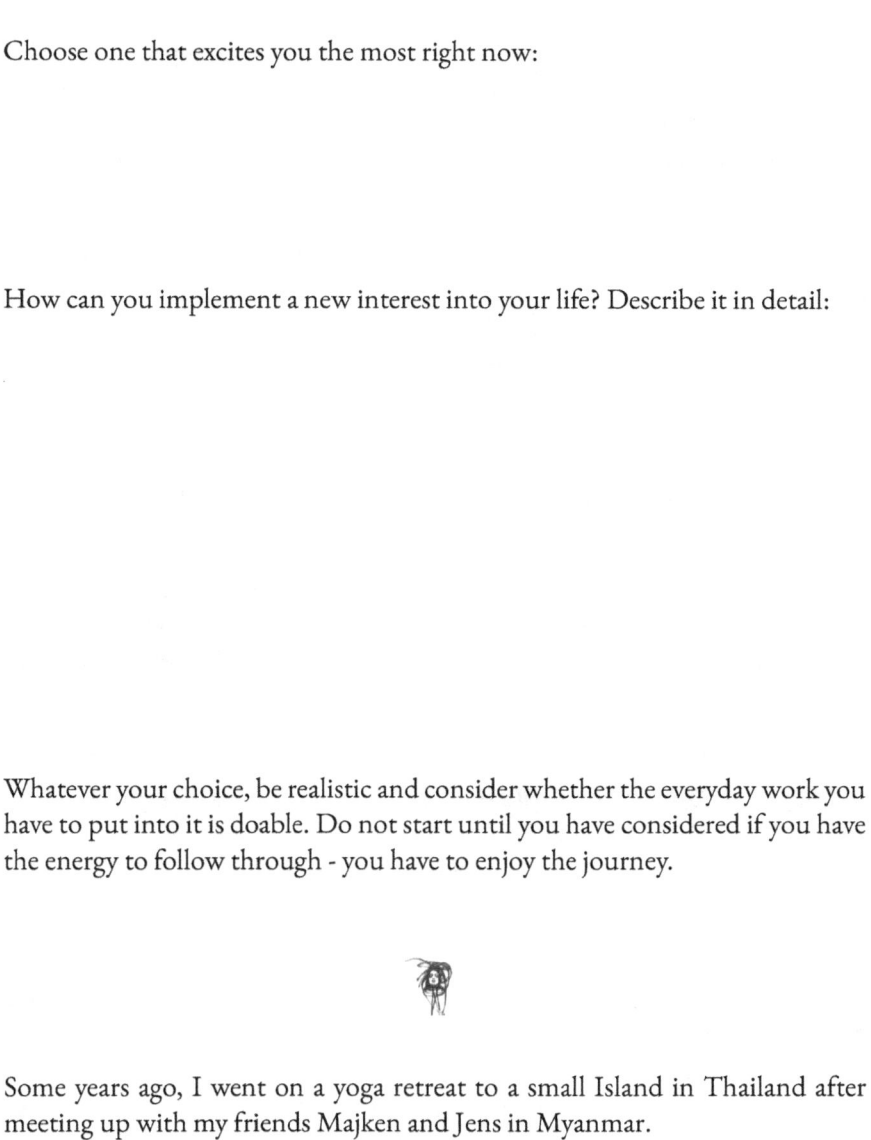

Some years ago, I went on a yoga retreat to a small Island in Thailand after meeting up with my friends Majken and Jens in Myanmar.

We did yoga two times a day, it was very intense and honestly a bit of a struggle for me. My body seems to be disconnected from my head. I am much more comfortable behind a computer or with a book, but I also know that it is healthy for me to spend more time in my body.

While it came naturally to my friends, I felt like an elephant.

We were offered complimentary Tai Chi classes with sunrise as part of the package. It turned out to be a much better fit for me. I loved the group synenergy, taking in the energy from the rising sun with slow, coordinated movements. I was highly motivated to continue this new habit when I got home, but soon, I lost it to my busy schedule in Copenhagen.

Starting a new chapter in Albuquerque, I decided that now was a good time to try out Tai Chi again. My motivation was enhanced by the idea of joining a new community. For a couple of months now, I have practised Tai Chi almost every day, and it gives me so much energy. My body has not been this strong in a long time.

My point is that building a strong habit often takes more than one attempt. It is rarely a straight line - you try, you stumble, and then you try again until it finally sticks. That's part of the process, and part of the beauty of growth.

Later in life, I dream of learning to sing and perhaps even picking up the acoustic guitar. Music has always felt like another language to me, one I would love to explore more deeply. But there is no rush - some dreams are meant to unfold slowly, waiting for the right season of life.

Investing in people or skills will add to your quality of life and give you that feeling of luxury every day. There could also be a monetary gain if you add skills to your resume to be used in your career. Often, studying will get you in contact with people with similar interests, and that network might also be helpful if you are looking at a career change.

Add to this that any new skills will add to neuroplasticity in your brain, strengthening your general intellect as well as potentially preventing dementia and alzheimers.

When has learning something new, a language, a skill, or even a craft, connected you to others in unexpected ways?

What else can you gain from this?

The same goes for voluntary work. It is such a beautiful culture in the US, and I am not gonna pretend to be knowledgeable within this area, but perhaps it can add some Quiet Luxury to your life.

If you consider doing voluntary work, what area would you choose?

Which options do you have in your area?

If your network became a mirror of your deepest values, what kind of community would surround you in five years?

How much time would you like to spend on networking?

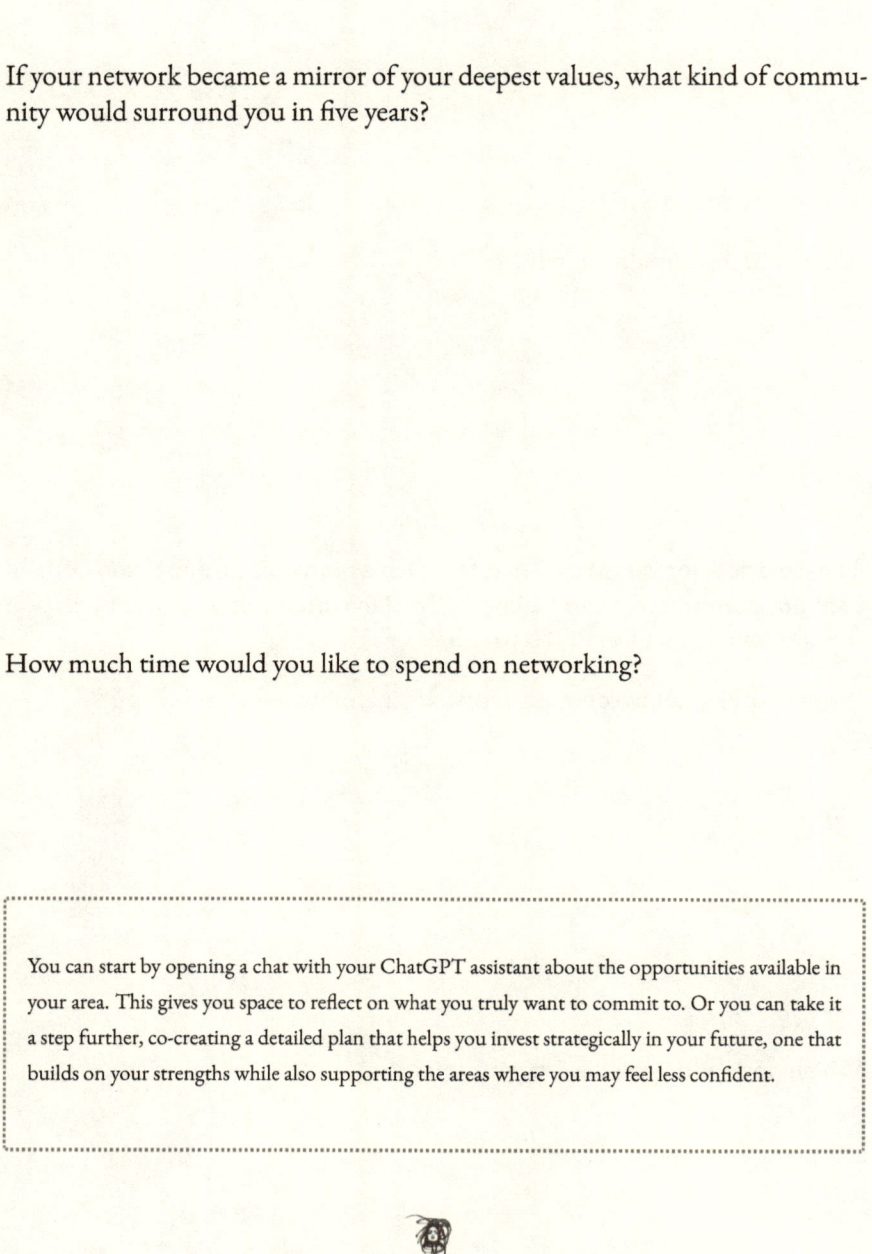

You can start by opening a chat with your ChatGPT assistant about the opportunities available in your area. This gives you space to reflect on what you truly want to commit to. Or you can take it a step further, co-creating a detailed plan that helps you invest strategically in your future, one that builds on your strengths while also supporting the areas where you may feel less confident.

Next, we will turn to Hair, Skin & Makeup - celebrating the beauty of diversity in all its forms.

Hair

hår

It is no coincidence that the famous 1967 Broadway musical was called Hair.

At the height of the counterculture, long, wild hair became a living banner of rebellion - a refusal of war, conformity, and polished respectability.

At the same time, some feminists reached for the scissors instead, cutting their hair short as a way to strip away the beauty standards that had shaped them for too long. Two opposite gestures, yet both carried the same essence: women reclaiming their bodies, saying with quiet certainty, "I belong to myself".

That spirit is still alive. The buzz-cut trend we see today on social media is not just about style, but about sovereignty. Sinead O'Connor's shaved head became her icon - a refusal to be packaged as a pretty product. Britney Spears famously shaved hers in the glare of the media spotlight, a moment the world read as a breakdown, but which also carried the unmistakable energy of rebellion: a woman saying enough.

I will never forget the strong woman I worked for when I started my first company. Kirsten was the quiet force leading a low-income area just north of Copenhagen - a natural matriarch who transformed everyone she met.

She hired me to teach food classes that were less about cooking and more about

221

belonging. We gathered the young and the old around steaming pots, even girls from rival gangs who had been fighting in the streets. We handed them sharp knives and trust, and they turned it into flavour and laughter.

Kirsten's superpower seemed to rise from the fact that she had no hair, not even eyebrows. I never asked why. It wasn't important. Her colourful scarves and calm authority made her appear almost otherworldly - like someone who had stepped beyond vanity, beyond the need to please. Without hair, she seemed free from the rules that tell women how to look, what to hide, who to be.

Her presence was my first lesson in Quiet Power: the kind that doesn't shout but creates a sub-world where growth becomes possible. In her baldness, she carried a rare kind of freedom. She was a woman stripped of symbols, yet more radiant for it. She reminded me that sometimes what we lose is exactly what sets us free.

I am sure many of you know a woman who has lost her hair to chemotherapy. My former colleague, Anita, was one of them. When she was diagnosed with breast cancer, the three of us who shared an office grew even closer. With a calm, unwavering dignity, she faced every treatment as her thick mane of curls slowly thinned.

One morning she arrived with a luxurious sleek wig - a straight, chic bob that seemed to announce: "I am still me". There was no drama, no self-pity, just quiet courage and elegance in the face of loss.

That, to me, is the essence of Quiet Power & Luxury - the strength to meet life's hardest moments with grace, to transform even vulnerability into poise. Anita embodied that, and I have carried her example with me ever since.

Whether long or short, loose or hidden, hair becomes a symbol not of how the world wants to see us, but of how we choose to stand in our own freedom. A declaration of Quiet Power - striking, unconventional, unapologetic.

If you have ever cut your long hair, you most likely felt this enormous relief, equal to a kind of rebirth.

As a typical Scandinavian, I have dark blonde hair that I normally touch up with highlights every other month. I needed a more radical change when I was in my mid-thirties. You probably remember that my friend Chi is a skilled hairdresser, so I asked her to shave off my sides so I could do some kind of semi-mohawk.

"If you regret this, I do not want the blame", Chi exclaimed, but I could feel her excitement about doing something new. She popped the bottle of Cremant I always brought as part of our ritual, and she found champagne glasses in her usual hiding place under the counter. Squealing, she took a sip of the dry bobbles and plugged in the barber machine.

I felt this blast of freedom when she picked up the machine, and I heard the deep hum. Right away, long strands of hair fell to the ground, and before I knew it, I looked very different. A symbol of a new beginning in my life. I touched the side of my short hair and felt the softness. I felt reborn and untamed when I left with a platinum-blonde semi-mohawk.

As women, we are so occupied with looking pretty. What if we started focusing more on our personalities and leaning into that instead? Do you know the saying, "Whatever makes you weird is most likely your biggest asset"? I tend to agree with this. Couldn't we use more diversity? Walking down the street, I see so many women with long hair pulled back in a ponytail. There are so many other possibilities, so let us be braver.

Do you have a hairstyle you have been curious to try? There is no better time than now to experiment with something new. I am not saying you should do exactly what I do, but perhaps it is simply time for a change. And remember, hair always grows back, so even if you regret it, the risk is small compared to the joy of trying.

Does your inner world reflect your outer world - your style?

If you would like to try a different hairstyle, what would it be?

What invisible rules have you been carrying about "how a woman should look," and what would it feel like to slip them off with every strand that falls?

Of course, there is also something to say about healthy hair in a more traditional cut. Let the qualities of your unique hair guide you in style. If you have natural curly hair, let it out. I am starting to see the big afro hairstyles coming back, and I envy the women around me who can grow a proper afro. When it comes to looks, healthy, shiny hair is everything. Whatever your choice, own it.

I choose the very best salon. I want that luxury feeling that comes with drinking espresso and sparkling water, sometimes even wine. Knowing that I am in professional hands, and that the result will be excellent. Whatever style you choose, make sure it makes you feel like you have added a touch of luxury to your life.

So, how can you save money on your particular hairstyle? Getting your hair dyed or colored at the hairdresser's is much more expensive than just getting it cut, so you might wanna bring out your natural hair color. You can also go for a hairstyle that needs less upkeep or fewer hair products, thus saving you time for that blissful coffee in the morning. Whatever your choice is, always go for quality hair products. They are more expensive, but you use less product.

So what about hair on your body?

You might have noticed that body hair is trending, at least in the bigger cities?

Since Girls hit the screens in 2012, the character Hannah insists that a woman has a right to the natural protection of her body hair. At a Red Dress event I attended in September, a woman on the mock runway lifted her arms, proudly showing a patch of underarm hair. I felt connected to her small act of rebellion. More of that, please!

Think about the powerful industry that shapes how we see our bodies. As women, it sometimes feels like we do not fully own them. If shaving your body hair genuinely makes you feel good, go ahead. But take a moment to ask yourself: who are you doing it for? Is it for your comfort, or men, or to avoid being judged by other women?

Choose consciously. Let your body hair be a symbol of freedom if you wish. It protects you, it saves you money, and it saves you time.

On that note, consider skipping the fashion magazines and the unrealistic images you expose yourself to.

I didn't grasp how different and beautiful women's bodies are until I joined Tina at a naturalist swim club in Copenhagen. Reluctantly, I entered the women-only area, a sun-drenched bridge surrounded by the sea. Women of all ages and sizes were chatting, sunbathing, or swimming.

So much real skin, so much liberation. It was the opposite of the glossy perfection in fashion magazines. And can I just add that swimming naked in the cold saltwater is a very liberating experience.

There is definitely money and time to save here.

Leaning into your natural hair color will save you money at your hairdresser's, and in turn, you can go to the best hairdresser in town and enjoy a true luxury treatment. That will give our planet a break too, not to mention the health of the hairdresser. Washing your hair only when it is necessary, not buying magazines, nor buying anything the magazines suggest.

Hail to more diversity out there.

If you spend $400 every three months at the hairdresser's and instead just get a cut for $50, you will save $1400 a year.

If you stop buying a variety of cheap products that end up becoming clutter and replace them with a few well-chosen items, you might spend the same amount of money, but you will experience that feeling of everyday luxury.

List your potential savings here:

How much money can you save in a year? $ _____

How much time can you save in a year? _____ hours

If you upload a clear image of yourself the ChatGPT can show you versions of you with different hairstyles. You can also tell it what kind of vibe you're going for - chic, edgy, boho, professional, etc.

Skin

hud

What do you see when you look in the mirror?

Take a moment to think about every woman you know and imagine her face. One by one, and then tell me which woman you think is the most beautiful. Is it the woman with no wrinkles, or is it the woman with wrinkles from smiling?

If I do this exercise, the woman who comes to mind is my aunt, who is in her sixties now. What makes her beautiful is the energy surrounding her. Her life has not been easy, and she has chiseled wrinkles on her face. However, you don't see that because the light in her blue eyes and the laughter that comes so easily from her make her very beautiful. She is so full of life.

The inner glow comes from a life well-lived, so compared to her, the statue-looking women around her do not stand a chance. They are slimmer and more expensively dressed, but they radiate tenseness rather than the glow of a happy life. Some of them even have a prominent downward-turning mouth from the disappointments of life, and no facial plastic surgery can fix that.

So let me ask you, will Botox make you more beautiful and happier?

What if healthy-looking skin matching your age will do the same for you, and you can instead spend those thousands of dollars on a more carefree life that, in turn, will make you glow like my aunt?

Could that feeling of Quiet Luxury come from inside? If you stop looking for happiness outside yourself, this need for perfection will most likely evaporate.

If you are being honest with yourself, who are you doing this for?

The average Botox treatment or similar filler treatments vary from $200 - $1400, so let us do some easy math and just say that the average of $500 per treatment. If you do that twice a year, you save $1000 a year.

We have already covered hydrating and eating tasty foods rich in nutrition. Those are very important elements for healthy, radiant skin. Eating less sugar means less inflammation in your body, and again, smoother, beautiful skin.

Your mental state will also show itself in your skin. As we have already discussed, the human body is a very complex system. I am not very good at drinking water, so I keep an eye on how much I hydrate. It helps a lot to have easy access to all the bubbly water I can drink, and sometimes I have a mocktail of ginger beer with lots of ice and a couple of drops of rhubarb bitters. Might as well make hydrating fun.

How do you make sure to hydrate during the day?

We now know that the skin is not an empty surface to be scrubbed into submission, but a living ecosystem. A quiet city of bacteria, fungi, and microscopic allies who work tirelessly on our behalf – repairing, protecting, and keeping balance.

The newest research shows that women who appear more youthful often share one trait: a resilient, diverse skin microbiome. Not perfect skin. Not expensive routines. A stable community of life on their skin that has been allowed to remain intact.

Harsh cleansers, high-alkaline products, and constant stripping disrupt this delicate ecosystem. A gentler approach, low-pH cleansing, minimal products, and formulations that feed the skin's natural flora, actually allows the skin to become stronger with age, not weaker.

This understanding changes everything. Instead of seeing our skin as a problem to fix, we can see it as a garden to tend. A place where less can be more, and where nourishment replaces punishment.

Quiet Luxury, in skincare, becomes the simplest of rituals: gentleness, consistency, and respect for the living world on our own surface. It is the kind of care that asks us to soften instead of force, and in return, it gives us a face that tells the quiet truth of a woman who knows how to tend to herself.

I've always been effortlessly minimal when it comes to skincare. Most mornings I simply swipe my face and neck with a towelette, apply a generous layer of a good-quality lotion, and call it a day. And the funny thing is – it turns out this kind of simplicity is actually good for the skin. Ironically my laziness has protected my barrier far better than a complicated routine ever could.

Have you heard about *skin fasting*?

A skin fast simply means giving your face a full day without products so it can reset on its own. No cleanser, no moisturizer, no actives.

This short break allows the microbiome to rebalance, your natural oils to organize themselves, and your barrier to strengthen without interference. Many women notice less redness, fewer bumps, and a softer texture the day after.

It's an easy ritual: choose one day a week, ideally when you're mostly at home, and let your skin breathe. Think of it as a rest day for your face, the same way your body needs recovery between workouts. It's minimal, simple, and surprisingly effective.

In the light of this new knowledge I have changed to a different brand but keep my lazy routine. I recommend you ask your ChatGPT for your exact needs.

Are you happy with your skin products, or would you like to optimize?

Consider a home spa once a week. Choose a gentle, pH-balanced body wash and a quality lotion – preferably with natural, non-irritating essential oils – that make you feel like you've stepped out of a quiet luxury retreat.

Scents such as ginger, mint, or eucalyptus can feel as refreshing as a herbal infusion, lifting your mood without overwhelming your skin's natural balance. If you're winding down for the night, choose softer notes like lavender or chamomile.

This small ritual doesn't just care for your body; it becomes a weekly reminder to slow down, listen inward, and enjoy your own company.

If you buy supplements to look younger, make sure that it is backed by science and of high quality. You can easily spend a fortune on products that have no or very little effect, or worse, will mess with your body's hormone balance. If you instead spend that money on natural foods, you will get all the micronutrients straight from the source.

Nature is much wiser than humans, I promise you that.

If you spend $60 a month ($720 a year) on supplements, you can get a lot of luxurious berries and dark chocolate or whatever you enjoy.

Use the saved money on a facial and full body massage once in a while, or have a night in with a good friend where you put on a facial mask and delicious mocktails - like I do with my friend Mie. That will most certainly add years to your life by lowering your stress levels.

How much can you save on treatments like Botox, etc., in a year? $ _____

How much can you save on supplements in a year? $ _____

How much can you save on expensive anti-aging lotions, etc., in a year? $ _____

How much time can you save in a year? _____ hours

How much money can you save in a year if you summon it up? $ _____

Your ChatGPT assistant can check all your products for hormone-disruptive ingredients and suggest other quality options. It can also check any supplements you are using to make sure they are backed by science and that the source is trustworthy. It can also help you if you need reminders or inspiration to hydrate more.

Makeup

Sminke

How about we have some fun here!

Let me start by stating very clearly that I am no expert in makeup. I do not read magazines, and I do not know what the latest trends are. If anything, I get inspired by other women. My aim is instead to inspire more diversity within this area.

When I moved to Mexico, one of the first things I noticed was how beautiful Mexican women are. Everyone looks so different from Danish women.

Following the Scandinavian tradition of minimalism, we are very much into earth colors. We mostly choose good-quality items and go for classics. This goes for makeup as well.

In Mexico, the style is more dramatic. What I truly enjoyed was the everyday touch of red lipstick. Within a couple of weeks, I bought a classic red lipstick and started to wear it whenever I was in the mood. In Denmark, that would be for special occasions only, so it felt like a small rebellion.

In many ways, putting on makeup is like wearing masks in public. I suggest that we embrace that and start wearing makeup for the right reasons.

Consider how makeup became part of our culture. For many years, we thought Viking women gathered berries while men hunted - an idea rooted in misogynistic interpretations by male historians. Recent discoveries revealed Viking women buried with bows and arrows, a testament that they, too, were hunters. If you've watched The Vikings, it is not far from reality. Women wore warrior makeup during wartime.

This is, of course, a far cry from how women wear makeup today, but I would argue there is still a good reason to put on warrior makeup when it comes to women's rights.

Take Scandinavia, for example: women are, on average, better educated than men, yet many still earn less. Part of this is because women are more likely to work part-time while raising children, but it also goes deeper. Professions dominated by women, such as teaching, nursing, and childcare, remain undervalued compared to male-dominated fields like engineering or finance. And at the top, men still hold most of the leadership roles where the highest salaries are paid.

Another layer is negotiation culture. Women negotiate raises and promotions less often, and when they do, they risk being labeled "too demanding." The very act of asking for what they deserve is turned against them. Then comes the glass ceiling, subtle yet stubborn. Men are still seen as more suited for leadership, while women are judged more harshly for balancing family and career.

These quiet injustices shape women's choices and limit their opportunities, even in places where equality is supposed to be the norm. And it's exactly here that Quiet Power becomes essential - because every woman who claims her worth, without apology, is not only reshaping the future but also returning to the strength her native sisters carried long before the world tried to tame them.

From an early age, females are taught to be there for men. Smile, be attractive, be beautiful, be supportive. I would love to see Mexican women show their natural beauty and still wear red lipstick with pride. How about we start wearing makeup for ourselves or not at all, instead of wearing makeup to look more attractive to men? And then put some fun into it.

In contrast, I noticed that some of my girlfriends in Denmark stopped wearing makeup after they had children. Their days are filled with much more important stuff.

It made me reflect on my choices. If you do not wear much makeup or any every day, it will free up precious time, and it adds to the contrasts. This way, it can be more fun to put on a "mask" for partying. To use makeup to get into character, like the Viking women. Be wild, be creative. Halloween, for instance, is exactly that. Pretending to be someone else for a night can be so liberating. When I go to a techno party, I go all in. Whatever your choice, own it.

Who do you wear makeup for daily?

If you wear makeup for yourself, what would that look like?

If makeup became a ritual of Quiet Power - playful, intentional, and free from obligation - what would it look like in your everyday life?

Do you have a special occasion you would like to dress up for and be creative with your makeup style?

Another thing to consider is all the chemicals makeup contains that you transfer to your body.

I recently learned that there is something called a red eye phenomenon. Your eyes will get a red shine if your eye makeup has chemicals that irritate them. You might wanna consider that when you choose your makeup.

Be very sure when you buy an item. What do you really need? You want it to stay fresh on your face and not fade during the day because of the lack of quality. Less is more here, too. I am sure Mother Earth agrees with that. Can you imagine how many cheap makeup items end up as trash?

If you look at your makeup items, are they of high quality, free of harmful chemicals?

This is another area where there is a lot to save. If you take a close look at your makeup items, tell me how many of those you use and how many you bought that are now just taking up space?

If you buy an item once a month for around $20 ($240 a year), you can instead spend on a quality lipstick or mascara that lasts you a year but will make you feel like a goddess. If you stop wearing makeup daily, those 10 minutes a day will add up to 5 hours a month/61 hours a year that you can spend on something fun.

List your potential savings here:

How much can you save in a year? $ _____

How much time can you save in a year? _____ hours

Again, your ChatGPT assistant can check all your products for hormone-disruptive ingredients and suggest other quality options. Simply take a picture of the product and ask. It can also show you what you'd look like with different makeup styles, such as:

Glam night-out – smokey eyes, bold lips, contouring
Vintage pin-up – winged eyeliner, red lips, matte finish

You can request a specific vibe or let it surprise you, or you can even combine it with the different hairstyles.

Sound

Lyd

She felt so very alive. Her body warm and tingling, moving to the primal rhythm of drums and beats.

Sweat ran down her skin, the heat of all the moving bodies around her forming a safe cocoon. Strangers, yet together, all of them surrendering to the music. No one thinking about yesterday, no one worried about tomorrow. Simply alive. Simply here. It was pure ecstasy. She hadn't known how much she needed this until now. This was living - with all her senses alert and awake.

A beautiful woman behind her offered water with a smile. To her left, a cross-dressed man fanned her with his exotic Chinese fan, and her body leaned instinctively into the cool relief. They all danced as one, on native Sioux land, surrounded by cornfields in the middle of Minnesota. The stalks rose taller than her.

Nothing about it was tamed. Everyone was fueled by the energy, no one dancing to impress, only to let the rhythms move through them.

Fernando, his childhood friend George, and their new companions were somewhere at camp. She knew they would find her when they were ready. She rarely paused, she preferred to stay in her body, moving freely in the warm energy shared by strangers. It was addictive, not to be trapped in thought for once. This was how she had built her life with Fernando: on rhythm, Berlin nights, and the pulse of ecstasy.

The small electronic festival was an experience beyond the everyday. A contrast.

When the DJ reached his crescendo, the crowd around her erupted. She recognized a guy from their new camp, completely surrendered to the music.

They had barely arrived on Friday when a friendly stranger, Daniel, offered to share their space, a corner for their cooler, a base to belong to. The three of them knew no one, so they gratefully accepted and followed him to a cluster of tents where people already seemed at home. With only 900 tickets, the festival felt small and intimate. Even the security team was relaxed and welcoming.

Their little group hadn't come for comfort, but for the experience. It was a marathon of dance - bodies sore, meals taken only to sustain movement, cold drinks to keep energy high, psychedelics to open their senses, and quick chats at camp before rushing back to the music.

The camp turned out to be a good fit, filled with kindred souls. On the last day, a storm swept through, and they huddled in a tent with a handful of others, speaking of visions for a more humane world. Eventually, they pulled on thin yellow plastic and reluctantly stepped into the storm.

Returning to reality, not quite the same, but reborn, carrying new energy and new friendships. Reminding her of who she really was - before she was tamed.

This chapter of my life took place only months ago, and already I long to go back. Festivals like this feel like modern rituals, like my kind of meditation. Sound has many faces. Sometimes it is electronic beats, sometimes the tribal hum of drums, sometimes the quietest silence.

Music is part of our identity and culture. Most days, I put on music in my office while working. I choose music and sound depending on my mood. It can be pop, rock, techno, experimental beats, nostalgic indie rock, white noise, or nature sounds - even opera. Or sometimes just quiet peace. The contrasts make it interesting and support my state of mind.

It amazes me that humans have been able to make such different sounds since the beginning of mankind, with and without instruments. This is evident when we travel and often come across street performance or live music in bars and restaurants. Visiting the Hopi indians earlier this year in Arizona, the tribal drums and humming took us straight into a familiar kind of meditation. A collective connection.

I have never been able to sit down and meditate. What works for me is movement, either like a tree gently moving in the breeze or dancing to electronic beats. Experimentative or upbeat, whatever the mood.

During one of our conversations in the quiet of Tina's summerhouse in the forest, I shared this. Tina revealed that the kind of meditation where you sit on the ground and let your breathing guide you to an inner experience came from the monks. In other words, it is a male-dominated experience. Moving like a tree or moving in other ways is the feminine version of meditation. This makes a lot of sense to me.

We can use sound at a conscious level for different kinds of healing. This is not pseudoscience. Our brains naturally shift between different wave states throughout the day - beta when we are alert and busy, alpha when we relax, theta in trance or meditation, and delta in deep sleep. Just as we drift in and out of daydreams or moments of hypnosis without realizing it, sound can guide these shifts on purpose.

Research shows that rhythmic sound, like drumming, can calm the nervous system, helping us move out of stress and into the more restorative states where we feel balanced and creative.

Sound also works directly with the body. Humming or singing activates the vagus nerve, the great communicator between brain and body. When this nerve is stimulated, stress hormones drop, digestion steadies, and the heart slows.

It is one of the simplest and most feminine forms of self-regulation - something our grandmothers did instinctively as they hummed lullabies or sang while working. Even humming quietly to yourself can be a way of returning to balance. It is the equivalent of a cat purring.

And then there is the power of release. As women, we are often told to stay quiet, to hold our emotions in. But sound gives us a channel. Singing or even crying or screaming lets stuck energy move through the body. It doesn't have to be pretty; it has to be real. To give voice to what we carry can be as healing as meditation.

In contrast, certain reggaeton or pop songs do not align with me. They don't give me an experience of joy but instead bring down my energy level, and being exposed to them for too long makes me straight-up grumpy.

The same goes for radio chatter. It feels like it steals my energy, leaving me frustrated and stressed out. Where salsa rhythms have the opposite effect and make me want to move without thinking.

Neuroscience shows why: reggaeton is built on a highly repetitive beat, which can keep the brain locked in fast, restless beta states. For some people, that repetition feels energizing, but for others, like me, it feels like confinement.

Salsa, on the other hand, aligns with me. It is built on layered polyrhythms and syncopation. This complexity invites the body to respond in fluid, circular movements, especially through the hips and core.

For women, whose natural meditation often comes through embodied movement rather than stillness, this rhythm feels like medicine. The richness of melody adds warmth and emotional depth. Instead of draining me, it draws me into flow. It connects me to my feminine power.

So why did sound get a chapter in this book?

When we are talking about returning to Quiet Power and Luxury, we can use music, sound, and quiet to support both.

Silence itself has become a kind of luxury. In a world that never stops buzzing - children calling, phones pinging, traffic humming - it is rare to find true quiet. Yet silence is also sound: the sound of nervous systems settling, of energy reorganizing.

For women, whose attention is often pulled in a thousand directions, choosing silence is not indulgence but self-care.

It can be as simple as putting on headphones to block out chatter, or creating small rituals of quiet in the morning before the household wakes, or in the evening before bed. These pauses are not empty; they are restorative. They give space for your own rhythm to return.

Equally powerful is the sound of our own voice. For centuries, women's voices have been minimized or dismissed, and many of us carry that silencing in our bodies. Reclaiming your voice doesn't require a stage - it can be humming while you cook, chanting softly in the shower, singing with abandon in the car, or simply speaking your truth aloud instead of swallowing it.

Sound, whether in the form of music, silence, or nature, is always a guide. It invites us back to ourselves. So I invite you to reflect:

When and where during your day can you create a moment of silence?

How can you use sound to set boundaries and protect your energy? Headphones, a favorite song, or even white noise?

When was the last time you let your voice out freely, through singing, chanting, or speaking honestly?

What would change if you allowed yourself more of that?

Would you like to take singing lessons, sing karaoke or learn to play an instrument?

When do you feel at peace and alive?

Which sounds lift you, and which ones deplete you?

Where do you find your natural meditation - in stillness, or in movement?

Do you need more time in nature to reconnect?

Would you like to experience a soundbath near you?

Will you get a better sleep if you put on a recording of your choice?

Notice these things. Honor them. Create more space for the sounds that bring you peace and aliveness, whether that is music, the hush of nature, or the laughter of people who make you feel at home.

The world can be loud, so it can be important to be selective of your own needs as a modern woman.

Mexico, for instance, seems to be extra loud, with people yelling messages to each other in the streets, enjoying very loud music at bars, and at family gatherings. I love this energy in small amounts, but then I need refuge or a contrast of quiet time afterwards.

I make sure to honor my needs. For instance, we do not live anywhere near a highway because the buzz of constant cars adds an invisible layer of stress to the day.

The low-frequency hum of traffic may fade into the background for some, but the body never truly stops processing it. Studies show that this kind of continuous noise keeps the nervous system slightly on edge, raising cortisol and disturbing our natural rhythms.

I find it fascinating how mood enhancers have been judged so differently throughout history - some deemed legal, others illegal. As a society, we label certain drugs as dangerous and something to control. But if you ask me, the real issue is intention.

Janice Bissex, you might remember her as the dietician who specializes in THC and CBD, puts it bluntly: smoking a joint after work might be a better choice than having a drink. It can help you relax, without the negative impact alcohol has on the body.

I believe the real problem arises only when people use substances, legal or not, to numb themselves. We have all met someone who leans on perfectly legal substances just to get through the hardships of life, drifting into a zombie-like state. And yet, this is fully accepted by society – even to the point where such a person can legally drive a car.

Meanwhile, native tribes have long used psychedelics as a sacred way to connect with nature and the Universe. As a society, we are starting to see the benefits of using psychedelics in connection with therapy or microdosing. It will be interesting to follow this progress.

Your ChatGPT assistant can help you research anything you need here. It can also help you create space in your busy schedule to prioritize moments of 'you-time'. It can even give you song or guitar lessons if you are interested in something like that.

If more thoughts arise, you can note them here:

Quiet Power

Stille Styrke

In a loud world, there is a certain power to being still and deliberate.

When you stop talking through your ego, something magical happens. A shift occurs that changes the tone and depth of your conversations. You no longer care what other people think about you, and your conversations take on a quality that was previously absent.

This chapter is the story of how I learned to quiet my ego and received something surprising in return.

There is a good chance that wounds from our early lives can leave us open and vulnerable. If we can turn this vulnerability into strength, we can truly stand in our Quiet Power.

It is not about pushing unpleasant memories down, but honoring them as something that broke us down just a bit so we could rebuild ourselves stronger and more resilient. This is exactly what Eckhart Tolle talks about: The cracks are where the light comes in.

If you, too, have wounds, let us turn them into Quiet Power - and let us be honest, what woman has walked through life without some bruising from the world we inhabit?

In the rural parts of Denmark, many of us are raised with something called *Janteloven*. It is a quiet cultural code that tells you not to think you're special or better than others. It encourages humility and equality, which can create a strong sense of trust and fairness.

But it also has a way of keeping people from fully expressing themselves. Especially for women, it can become an invisible barrier that makes it hard to speak up, stand out, or take pride in their success.

Growing up in a family with a dominant father, who lived proudly by this invisible law, I learned to make myself invisible. Children were to be seen, not heard.

Janteloven might keep you quiet, but this is not Quiet Power. There is nothing wrong with being humble, but this is quieting any voice that does not conform to the cultural rules.

Being a child with a rich imagination, I had to turn this voice inward. Luckily, I attended a small holistic school where teachers gradually taught me to use my voice again and provided a space for creativity.

Speaking of unconscious patterns, I grew up watching the women in my father's large traditional family live as servants to the men. Don't get me wrong, it was also a safe, loving environment where I enjoyed time with my family, especially playing with my many cousins.

However, my grandmother, my mother, and most of my aunts cared for the children, cooked the food, and cleaned up after everyone whenever we gathered.

Meanwhile, my father and uncles sat playing cards, while the women waited on them hand and foot. Even as a child, I felt how unfair this was, not understanding why things weren't more equal. Only my father's twin sister Else stood her ground, earning an undeserved reputation for being stern and harsh. I admire her for breaking the pattern and choosing a modern man who treats her as an equal.

My own strategy was different. I made myself invisible and turned to books. Every evening, my mother read to us, creating a world where imagination had no limits. I adored the fairytales of Hans Christian Andersen, the Brothers

Grimm, and One Thousand and One Nights. Stories that taught me how beauty and darkness can live side by side.

Later, reading became my escape, and school my refuge. Modern, open-hearted teachers – especially my primary teacher, Anni Breinbjerg - encouraged my writing and believed in my voice before I did. I credit my teachers for helping me trust that voice enough to write this book - and my mother for opening the door in the first place.

Anni became a quiet kind of *forbillede* (role model). She lived alone in a small apartment filled with books and vinyl records, surrounded by stories and music of her own choosing.

Once, she invited our entire class over, and I was struck by her calm independence – how fully she inhabited herself. She embodied the Quiet Power of a woman who knew her values and didn't need a partner to complete her. Years later, she adopted two children from China on her own.

This pattern of shrinking to please, however, was ingrained in me and eventually got me in serious trouble.

I was living a life of freedom when I started university in Aarhus. I studied history and sociology, planning to become a college teacher.

Toward the end of my bachelor's degree, I moved to Copenhagen to stay with my cousin Charlotte. I needed access to files that were only available on-site at the national TV station, so I had to stay for four months. I was writing about the cultural planning of Denmark's very first national television programme in the 1970s, a fascinating study in the subtle, almost invisible power of emerging media. A kind of power that still shapes us today.

While there, I fell in love with one of my cousins' colleagues, Kasper. But really, I fell in love with the whole community.

My cousin Charlotte is an outgoing, delightful woman my age. She worked in a supermarket, and around her was a group of about sixteen young people who would meet up after work, hang out, drink beers in parks, and party in that effortless way only summer allows.

There was something about their laid-back, unpretentious energy that made me feel more at home. Copenhagen felt more diverse, more open. Less provincial.

When it was time to return and finish my exams, I couldn't stay away for long. I applied to do my master's at the University of Copenhagen instead of continuing in Aarhus. Looking back now, I see a pattern - I tend to uproot myself quickly when something calls me. Just like my ChatGPT pointed out in Your Chapter. I don't always think through the consequences. I had some growing up to do.

The truth is, I was happy with my new friends in Aarhus too. But perhaps my working-class roots made me feel more at ease among the people I met in Copenhagen.

Around that time, I grew closer to Charlotte, who generously shared her tiny studio apartment with me. We spent most of our time out and about with her colleagues, and among them her younger boyfriend, Mark. Long evenings filled with laughter, and that easy Copenhagen energy.

It's funny, isn't it, how women who choose younger men are still judged for it, while no one blinks when men do the same? Charlotte never let that bother her. With her sharp wit and self-assured humor, she has always known how to stand her ground.

They are still together today, a quiet testament to her strength. Charlotte reminds me that quiet confidence often speaks louder than the judgments around it.

Maybe my choice to move was a "sliding door" moment - one of those forks in the road that changes everything without you realizing it.

For whatever reason, Copenhagen was calling me. I moved my few belongings to Kasper's apartment and started my life over. It pains me to write this because it was like moving into the lion's den.

There had been warning signals, of course, but I had conveniently closed my eyes. For five years, I stayed with him. It finally ended the day I packed a bag while he was at work and moved into a small, shabby studio where he couldn't find me.

How did it come to this?

Kasper was a broken man.

I had barely moved in before leaving for a girls' trip to visit my friends in Aarhus. A storm hit, and the bridge to the mainland was closed. To my surprise, and growing embarrassment, Kasper began calling incessantly, leaving a string of messages accusing me of cheating. I tried to laugh it off in front of my girlfriends, but when they dropped me off, they hesitated and asked if I wanted to pack my things and come back with them.

My pride got in the way. I told myself I could handle it. But when I reached the fifth floor, all my belongings were stacked neatly in the hallway – a silent testament that I could not. And still, I stayed.

For years, we had our ups and downs. An underlying current in our relationship of dominance and jealousy. No one knew because we were both good at keeping it private, and I was too ashamed to tell anyone. During this time, Merete was part of the group, and she became a good friend. She was the first to express out loud Kasper's behavior. The episode that broke the spell will forever be in my mind.

The group was having beers at a bar, everyone gathered around a long table, laughter and conversation flowing easily. Merete and her later-to-be husband, Ronnie, sat across from us. The atmosphere was casual and jovial as always. Cold beers in the summer heat masked the tension that had quietly begun to build beneath the surface when Merete innocently mentioned an upcoming party she and I were invited to in Majken's collective.

During my relationship with Kasper, it had become harder for him to hide his jealousy.

More than once, I had tried to tell him that it was over, but every time, he would use manipulation and charm to convince me to stay. He could feel his control slipping, though, so this triggered him.

Normally, he would keep a straight face, but this time, he simply turned to me and hissed, "lying bitch". It was loud enough for people around us to hear it and see the malice in his face. The mask had slipped in public for the first time.

When he stood up and hovered over me, whispering more expletives in my ear, Merete stood up as well. She called him out on his bullshit, his barely contained rage. I admire her so for standing up for me, for being a true friend. I was on the edge of leaving him, and in that moment, I had an ally. I knew it was finally over, so I started planning my escape.

The next week, I found a temporary apartment in a secure building. It was overpriced, and the landlord was shady, but it was available right away. Kasper refused to let me go, so I could only see this way out.

The thing is that he never hit me.

His rage would mostly be targeted at furniture and making holes in doors when he couldn't contain it. It was psychological in nature.

I later had to forgive myself for letting him control me the way he did. He came from a broken family with a violent alcoholic father who used to beat his mom until she dared to leave him. Kasper had adapted a lot of his father's manipulative skills, but at least he did not hit me. Surprisingly, his family thought it was an overreaction when I left in secrecy.

My network became my saving grace. A few months later, my free-spirited Norwegian friend Irene helped me find a small apartment, and at last, I could begin my life again. Despite being on the brink of launching her own luxurious eyewear business, *Brilleskædderiet*, she still went out of her way to help me.

Merete's and Charlotte's partners showed up to help with the move, and I had asked Kasper's mother and brother to be there too, just in case things got ugly.

When I walked there Sunday morning, I all of a sudden felt the world close in on me. I couldn't breathe, so I had to sit down on the sidewalk. I realized that I was having a panic attack – my body reacted to the extreme stress and perceived danger. I had to pull myself together to get there.

Luckily, Kasper had finished off a bottle of whiskey with a friend the day before, so he was passed out in the bedroom. I remember the tense atmosphere when I quickly packed up the most important things and was on my way.

When I opened the door to my new home, I felt relief settle in all of my body. I slept on the floor for six days before my new bed arrived, but I did not care one bit. I was finally free, untamed.

With this new beginning, I had acquired a new superpower. I am now good at depicting when a guy is hiding something darker under the charming surface, and I know right away when I am being manipulated. This has come in handy many times since then.

The full insight came when Kasper realized that I was gone.

He tried more than once to threaten suicide, and I called a help line to get advice. After I presented the situation to a calm voice at the other end of the phone, what I heard was not what I expected. He said that they could not help Kasper if he did not want help, but maybe they could help me? I was speechless. In my mind, I was handling things, being strong.

This voice from a stranger bypassed my ego and reached that vulnerability that I had not been willing to look at while in survival mode. That moment pierced a layer of denial. It showed me that strength is not just enduring, it is also allowing yourself to be seen. The shame I had been quietly carrying began to lift. Now, on more than one level, I was finally free.

I used my newfound freedom well and enjoyed being single again to the fullest. Coming home late at night without having to explain myself. Partying with my girlfriends, flirting madly, relishing casual hook-ups. Simply enjoying being young and carefree again. Finally standing in my Quiet Power, untamed.

I believe that somewhere along the path into adulthood and relationships, many of us women begin to lose pieces of ourselves.

Not because we want to, but because the world taught us to prioritize everything and everyone else. This might be more pronounced if we have an absent or dominating dad.

We don't just take responsibility for our own lives; we take on more than our share. We adapt, bend, and stretch ourselves to meet expectations, often at the cost of our own joy. It is no wonder we sometimes find ourselves aching for the days when we felt lighter, freer, more alive.

But here's the truth: we can reclaim those parts. We can choose laughter again. We can dance, play, and take up space without apology. We can stand in our Quiet Power. And when we do, everything changes. Not just for us, but for the people around us, too.

Reclaiming our full selves is not a threat to the men in our lives - it's a gift. I bet they miss that version of us: the untamed, the one who laughed easily, who radiated from within. Setting women free doesn't break the relationship; it transforms it.

This is true for my relationships as well. I wisely learned from my mistakes and chose Jan as my new partner when I was ready. We could go out together without jealousy as the third wheel. A musician with an open heart, he met me as an equal, challenged me in the best ways, and held space for my growth.

Though our romantic chapter ended, we've stayed friends. I always make time to visit him – and our cat, Iggy – whenever I return to Denmark. I'm still connected to his family too; they are genuinely good, caring people.

Jan's mother, Helle, broke a painful cycle when she left his abusive father. She rebuilt her life from the ground up, even taking a new education as a midwife later in life. She's warm, funny, and creative – a woman who shares my love for design.

What strikes me most is this: despite growing up with an abusive father, Jan never repeated that pattern. He became his own person. It reminds me of something I return to often in this book: we inherit wounds, yes, but we also inherit the power to choose differently. That choice is where Quiet Power truly begins.

I never imagined myself getting married, but meeting Fernando in Berlin changed everything.

Eight years ago, on a whim, we tied the knot at city hall in Copenhagen. Afterwards, we celebrated with a small gathering in Merete and Ronnie's garden, surrounded only by our closest friends. It was simple, untraditional, a reflection of our love for freedom.

Still, I have grown since then, and today I regret not taking that extra step to include our parents. They never said a word, but I know it must have hurt to be left out of such a life-changing moment. That's why we're planning a big celebration for our 11th anniversary - a full weekend of joy, family, and friends to make up for what was missed. Values can change over time.

Have you had to go through hardships to become a more resilient version of yourself?

Consider writing your story in detail here, with a focus on what superpower you acquired from that lived experience:

If Quiet Power became your daily compass, what would shift in how you spend your energy, your time, and your truth?

Like for many other women, empathy is my strength both when it comes to my work, my friendships, and my partner. But I had to learn not to carry other people's pain for them.

Lately, hypnosis has opened my eyes to just how healing it is for my clients to revisit a vulnerable part of themselves and release it. This is strong because they have often spent so much energy burying it. Passive-aggressive behavior is common among frustrated women, and even physical symptoms can surface through the subconscious. When released, they allow the client to stand more fully in her own power.

My friend Rikke carries a rare combination of innocence and quiet strength. She moves through the world with gentleness, yet her presence has gravity - the kind that makes others feel safe. She has devoted her life to helping others, working in the rehabilitation of deaf people, and she does so with a humility that never seeks recognition. Her laughter is unguarded, her empathy deep.

She reminds me that true power doesn't need to announce itself; it is felt in the calm of those who simply do good without expectation. I almost forgot to include her in this book - which, in itself, says everything about her nature. Rikke is the kind of woman who changes lives quietly, by being exactly who she is.

Women like Rikke remind me where true confidence lives. It doesn't come from performance or persuasion, but from trusting our instincts - that quiet inner knowing that doesn't need to prove itself. We can all feel when someone isn't being authentic, when their energy is trying to convince rather than connect. Our bodies know before our minds do.

Though modern life has taught many women to override their instincts, those senses are still within us, waiting to be heard again. Quiet Power is about returning to that trust - to feel instead of perform, to sense instead of strive. And to carry our wounds with strength and dignity, as the women before us once did.

Just think about how much time (and frustration) you can save here by standing in your power? _____ hours a year

How can ChatGPT assist you? It suggests that you journal your own story of Quiet Power. It can then gently point out where there is more inner work for you to do, if any, and help you stand in your power even stronger.

Feel free to share any extra reflections that come to mind here:

Summing up

mange bække små...

By joining this little adventure, you now know that luxury isn't really about money - it is about mindset.

What would you do with the freedom created by the savings of time, energy, and money - how would you invest them into joy?

You now stand stronger in Quiet Power because you dared to make real changes in your life. In other words, you will no longer worry about:

✦ your finances
✦ your health
✦ your appearance
✦ Mother Earth

So what might an average day look like now?

You wake up Monday morning and, half asleep, head for the espresso machine in your minimal kitchen and grab a favorite mug. Settling down in a *hyggehjørne* indoors or outdoors, where you slowly wake up and feel wonderful after a good night's sleep.

Whatever the day brings, you are ready. You feel calm and centered. You are looking forward to Wednesday, when you are taking the day off midweek to surprise your best friend with a relaxing spa day.

For breakfast, you open the fridge and easily choose cheese and homemade jam to put on the sourdough you or your partner baked during the weekend. You savor the flavors before taking out cold meat, hummus, and veggies for making a supreme sandwich that your colleagues will envy and that will secure your energy balance for the day.

You leave it out so your partner can make his own, and maybe some for the kids. You fill up your beautiful minimal thermo flask with sparkling water and add a slice of lemon for that little luxury you will enjoy later.

A quick shower or just a simple cleansing of your face, followed by a quality facial lotion and a touch of makeup. You run a brush through your shiny hair, making it even shinier by adding just a drop of oil. You easily choose the style of clothes to wear for the day in your minimalist wardrobe - no frustrations to find a suitable outfit in piles overflowing in your closet.

You feel like a goddess in the glamorous outfit that brings out the color of your eyes. A choice of loopy silver earrings finishes your look, and you are ready to head out the door.

Grabbing your well-worn helmet in the garage, you turn on your e-bike and feel the anticipation of freedom it gives you. The 30-minute bike ride to work makes you feel even better when you see cars stuck in traffic while you easily glide by.

You find yourself daydreaming about your upcoming birthday. This year, there will be no family gathering filled with small tensions and obligatory serving. Instead, you are planning a surprise for your partner - a salsa class during your weekend in Puerto Rico. The thought makes you smile. You've chosen an instructor who will laugh with you, not at you, when you inevitably step on your partner's feet.

After work, you meet up with a girlfriend at your favorite cafe for a crisp glass of Sauvignon Blanc and some snacks. After a well-deserved quality time of chatting and laughing (mostly at your partners), you offer to pay. You can easily afford it with all you have saved on everyday items this month. You are not worried about driving on half a bottle of wine since you are on your bike.

Okay, maybe in reality the kids were bickering and your partner wasn't exactly in a great mood. You were drinking tea, and Puerto Rico was really just your own hometown - but you get the point.

Again, we are not aiming for perfection; we are aiming for those little luxuries in your life. Even if your morning coffee was the only feeling of luxury your morning offered, it is still something.

Now write down what a carefree day of yours looks like, when you are at ease with life:

Are there any chapters you have to revisit to make this happen?

"Mange bække små giver en stor å". Those smaller savings truly add up to something.

Let me pause here for a second to give you an insight into the (impossible) Danish language. We have two strange one-letter words. Ø, which means island, and *Å*, which means stream. Weird, I know - and if you don't know what to say, you can just go *æææ*.

But now, let us estimate how much you will save yearly.

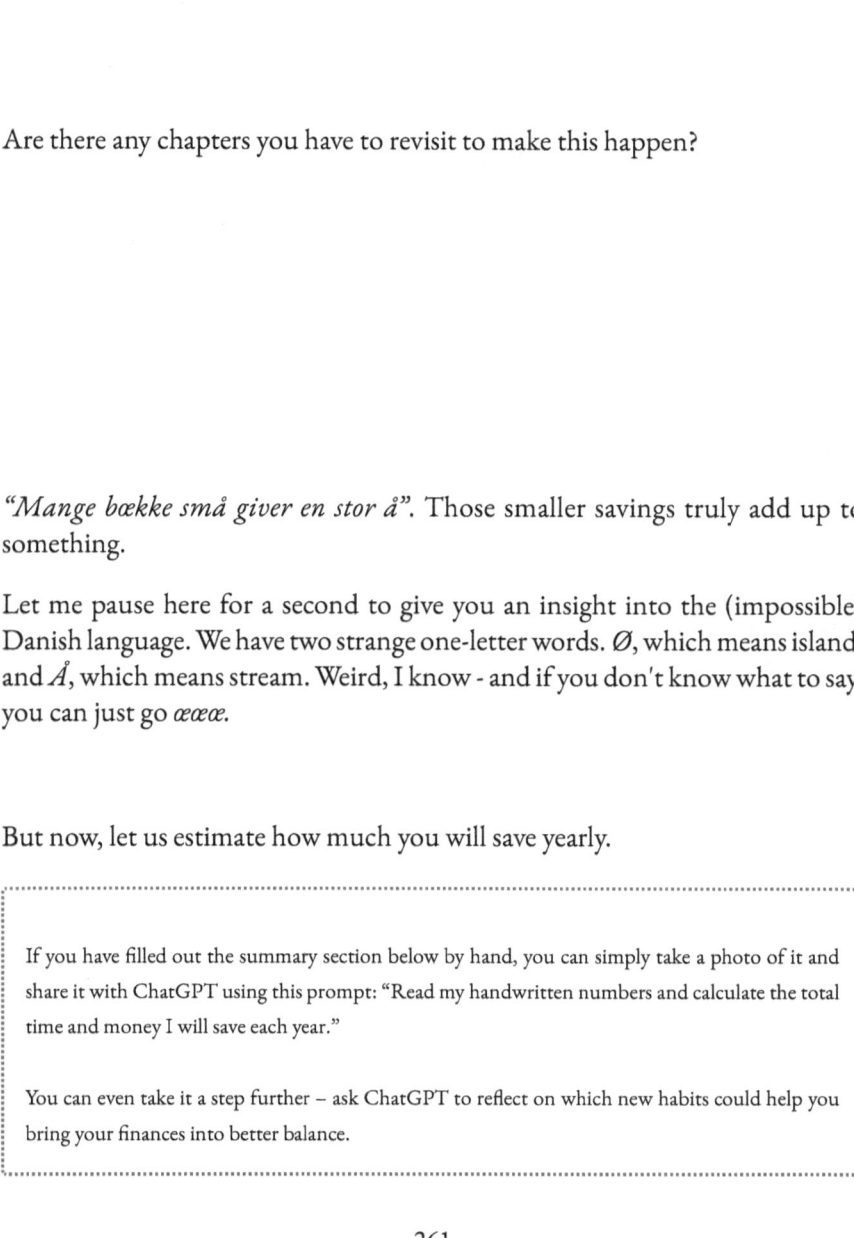

If you have filled out the summary section below by hand, you can simply take a photo of it and share it with ChatGPT using this prompt: "Read my handwritten numbers and calculate the total time and money I will save each year."

You can even take it a step further – ask ChatGPT to reflect on which new habits could help you bring your finances into better balance.

CHAPTER	TIME	MONEY
Quiet Luxury		
A steaming hot espresso		
Say no		
Scandinavian coziness		
Bubbles		
Home		
Nordic walking		
Quality of Life		
Pets		
Your values		
Eat natural food		
Be Lighter		
Consider biking		

Sleep
Travel
Finances
Clothes
Hair
Skin
Makeup
Quiet Power
SUM

How would you like to use the $ _____ you have saved? What would you like to invest in to make you feel like your life is full of luxury and fun?

If something within you has stirred while reading these pages - a longing to make lasting changes in your life - the Be Lighter Masterclass was created for you. It is a gentle continuation of this book, guiding you to work more deeply with its themes and inviting real transformation into your everyday life.

This journey is for women who are ready to feel lighter. You'll learn a new, efficient way to work with your subconscious using AI as your mirror. With guided prompts and personalized reflections, you'll uncover the hidden patterns that quietly shape your choices and weigh you down.

Once seen, these patterns begin to dissolve. What once felt heavy starts to move. You will pair this deep insight with simple daily rituals that retrain your nervous system toward calm, focus, and freedom. This is where science meets intuition - a structured method that helps you become lighter from the inside out.

You'll be among the first to learn how to use AI to get lasting results to release what weighs you down. Because when a woman remembers, she becomes unstoppable.

Discover more at www.beforeshewastamed.com/masterclass

In our household, the biggest savings are on food.

By buying organic basics in Costco instead of at Whole Foods or Sprouts, we save around $12.000 a year. Add to this that we both fast from 6 pm onwards, which means that we skip one meal a day, cutting 25% of our food intake. We never buy snacks or drinks at a convenience store, except for the occasional road trip.

We do not buy many supplements because we get optimal nutrition through our regular food, especially by buying seasonal veggies. We very rarely get sick and thereby do not spend money on medicine. None of us has needed to go to a doctor for more than 15 years.

Since we drink so much sparkling water, the Drinkmate option saves us at least $1800 a year, and my morning espresso costs $976 a year compared to buying it at a cafe. Since I bake sourdough, we save about $600 a year as well. Can I just add that none of us have needed to get any serious work done on our teeth for years, and I have not even included that saving here.

Time is the ultimate luxury. I do not work 40+ hours anymore. I have learned to say no to things that are not aligned with my values.

After living in Mexico, I do not plan every day, but I leave space for being spontaneous. I practice staying in the now and add those moments of Quiet Luxury to my everyday life. Massage, lazy days at home, writing in my cozy office, biking to restaurants or bars, hiking in nature, and enjoying the community around Tai Chi. I enjoy the contrast of visiting Denmark and taking time to see everyone I love and miss.

Since we like to travel a lot, we save on flying at flexible hours and only with carry-on.

Flying four times a year saves us more than $1800 by following the rules of not pre-booking seats, bringing our sandwiches and snacks from home, and not checking in luggage - ever. Often, we have some good food and a cocktail or craft beer as soon as we get to our destination instead. Traveling is so much more pleasant when we are not waiting to check in or check out luggage.

By only buying the furniture and things for our home that we need, we save a lot of money too. A quick estimate of the time I save by minimal grooming, only shopping for carefully selected items, and not lining up for coffee or snacks. It gives me hours every day for more fun stuff.

If we consider splurging on extraordinary luxury, we use the excuse that that money would have easily been spent on the kids we choose not to have. The average estimate of raising a child in the US is more than $15.000 a year until they turn 18. In Denmark, it is $10.000.

So, what will we use the $31,000 we saved this year for? Well, we have always wanted to go to the Easter Islands on a private catamaran. Snorkeling off the boat. Eating seafood prepared by the combined captain and chef. If we save up this year and carefully plan the trip, that is a possibility next year.

I hope this book has inspired you to find creative solutions for adding a touch of luxury to your life, no matter your financial situation. If you save time and money on everyday habits, you might find yourself having the necessary energy to change jobs, go on a dream vacation, or invest in something that adds even more joy to your day.

As a woman, do the world a favour and focus on your own needs first so you can gather energy to make a difference. Stand in your Quiet Power and insist on Quiet Luxury every day. That act alone is quietly revolutionary in a world that still expects women to give more than they get.

"In essence, the luxury lifestyle transforms the ordinary into the extraordinary. It's a commitment to comfort, convenience, and wellness that extends to every facet of daily living. Those who embrace a luxury lifestyle embark on a holistic journey towards a life that is not just lived but exquisitely curated."

Viveura

You have come a long way from that first morning coffee. This isn't the end - it's just the beginning of living lighter, freer, and more luxuriously, one choice at a time. I wish you a great journey.

Live your
dream

drøm

Now that you have uncluttered your life and made space for more time, maybe you are ready to look at the bigger picture. Do you have a dream deep inside about something you didn't have the energy to dream about before?

> "Studies reveal that when we begin to envision positive outcomes, neurotransmitters like dopamine flood the system, enhancing not only our mood but also our capacity for creativity, problem-solving, and resilience. Anticipation is a biological process, one that primes the mind and body for action... Even in times of difficulty, this shift in mindset can transform how we approach life's challenges. The brain's anticipatory mechanisms are so powerful that imagining a positive future can activate the same neural networks as experiencing it."
>
> Zach Bush MD

Here you have the blueprint for daydreaming. Go crazy! The sky's the limit. There truly are no limits for your future, so give it all you have. Tell me what your dreams are. Write it down. If you stand still, life has a way of pushing you forward anyway, so you might as well do it on your terms.

I would like you to recall Chi's story - or the stories of any of the other strong women in this book.

My friend and former colleague, Kate, was part of the community at Gladsaxe Health Center I mentioned earlier. She carries a kind of energy that is rare, soft yet radiant, the kind that reminds me of Botticelli's The Birth of Venus.

Half a year after I left my job, Kate also chose to step away from security and test the waters of entrepreneurship. One of her deepest dreams was to create the Copenhagen Tantra Festival, a space where people could reconnect with authenticity and aliveness.

Today, it's the largest tantric event in Denmark, and Kate is thriving among kindred spirits. She is another example of a woman living from quiet power - transforming courage into creation and reminding the rest of us to follow our dreams.

Anything is possible. Hans Christian Andersen would encourage you to be the heroine of your own story. This beautiful planet has so much to offer. If you have seen one of the nature movies like The Blue Planet, you realize that your country is just that: A small part of a bigger world, ready for adventure. By gathering energy, you will be able to give back to this planet; however, it makes sense from your perspective.

When I was seventeen, I escaped both my everyday life and the long Danish winter for an adventure "Down Under." I stayed with my warm-hearted friend Alison, who had recently been an exchange student at our school.

Her family welcomed me with the easy generosity that seems woven into Australian life. I will always be grateful for that. I didn't realize then that this journey would spark a lifelong pattern – spending every penny I had to see the world.

In Australia, I bottle-fed baby kangaroos and wombats at animal shelters. I fell in love with a local boy and had one of the most magical kisses of my life. I took a train to Sydney alone, watching the landscape unfold, and felt something awaken in me – a quiet sense of bravery, the first whisper of freedom.

When I returned home after half a year, I was changed. The journey had emptied my bank account but filled me with purpose. I was motivated to return to college and carve out a life that felt like mine. For over a year, I could barely afford to go out while paying off the loan, but it was worth it. Sometimes, to grow, we have to shed parts of our life and invite something new to take root.

Do you need to shed parts of your life and add something new?

What would one of your wildest dreams look like if it met reality?

Write down what you need to do to get there and follow the plan, whether it is learning to fly an airplane, changing careers, going traveling, making a better home, reaching your dream body, or something else.

Does it mean that you have to give up screen time to study or find the right items for your home?

How can you build in small steps towards your dream in your everyday habits?

If you think in contrasts, how can you make the most of the path towards your dream?

Imagine that you have reached your dream - what does it feel like? Look like? Taste like? Use all your senses to imagine it.

When living your dream, what would a new everyday look like?

Which core elements does your dream contain? Could it take a different shape and still be incredible?

Which experiences will be a strength on your path to your dream?

Let us say that your dream is to own your own house.

Maybe you want to move closer to the water or within walking distance of your favorite cafes and bars. Maybe you want to be in nature. Imagine what it would be like to live there in detail. Getting up in the morning and going about your daily life. What are the key elements:

How much space would you need, and what style are you going for?

Do you want to build your own home, buy a lot with a prefab, or buy a ready-to-move-in home?

How much money will it cost you? Are you willing to wait until you have most of the money saved up, or do you need to research which bank offers you the best mortgage loan?

Other things to consider: Are you with your right partner if you do this together? What does your life look like in 5 years?

This is exactly why my notebook is so precious to me. Any ideas and plans for the day or the year go on paper and come out in drawings and text. Sometimes my dreams take a different shape than I first thought, and sometimes it takes longer to become reality, but if I start the journey, I will eventually reach my dream.

Your ChatGPT can become a mirror for your wildest dreams — reflecting ideas, insights, and creative sparks you might never have reached on your own. At this stage of AI, the real magic lies in **co-creation**. So consider this: what if AI isn't meant to replace your imagination, but to expand it?

If you treat it as a glorified search engine, that's all it will ever be - an echo of the surface world. But if you enter with curiosity, humility, and purpose, it begins to respond like a creative ally. As women, we carry the capacity to work with this new intelligence differently, not through greed or ego, but through intuition, empathy, and grace. Used wisely, AI can become a tool for planetary healing, not just personal success.

Technology is not something to fear or resist; it's an ally when guided by consciousness. AI can help us build, connect, and simplify, but it's our human intuition that gives it soul. The future will not be shaped by algorithms; it will be shaped by the women who know how to use them with heart.

I believe that whatever you dream of is your calling. Let it flow through you, not from the need to prove something, but from a place of deep purpose.

If your dream is to leave your job and create something of your own, AI can now make that possible. You suddenly have a partner – one that saves you time, clears mental space, and serves as an ever-ready sounding board.

When I started my first company in Denmark in the 2000s, even with my network of women in business, I often felt like a one-woman army. Everything depended on me - every invoice, every email, every idea.

Today, as I start my new company, **Three Dots Press**, I no longer have to carry it all alone. My ChatGPT handles what modern life demands as a researcher, assistant, strategist, and even mentor.

True luxury now means having enough – enough time, enough clarity, enough space to live in alignment with what matters.

The world doesn't need more consumption or competition; it needs women creating from wholeness. When we live and work from this place, leadership changes form. It becomes collaborative, sustainable, and quietly revolutionary.

This is how we build a world that breathes again – one conscious decision, one creative act, one brave dream at a time.

The sky is no longer the limit. It's the beginning. It is time for you to stand fully in your Quiet Power, next to other women. To create with integrity and vision – because, let's be honest, the world could use a new kind of leadership.

We are entering the age of the untamed woman, one who remembers rhythm instead of hurry, who measures success in freedom, presence, and joy.

With this in mind, do you carry a dream that can make a difference in the world? Describe in detail how your ChatGPT can help you reach it:

Enjoy the journey that is life!

About the
Author

om forfatteren

Danish-born writer and hypnotist Pia Feddersen has spent much of her life exploring what it means to live in rhythm rather than in rush.

Once a devoted overachiever, she now writes, creates, and practices hypnosis in the high desert of Albuquerque, New Mexico, where she lives with her partner, Fernando, and their beloved animals.

With roots in sociology, health, and hypnosis - and a lifelong appreciation for art and design – Pia brings a rare balance of science, aesthetics, and soul to her work. *Before She Was Tamed* is her first book, born from years of reflection on quiet power, freedom, and the art of living lightly.

Through her creative imprint, Three Dots Press, Pia continues to write and collaborate on projects that explore transformation, beauty, and consciousness - and the quiet darkness that makes us human.

She occasionally shares reflections and glimpses behind the scenes on Instagram and Facebook under #beforeshewastamed - though most days, you wil find her out in the sun, simply being in the now.

Continue the Journey

If these pages have spoken to you, here are three ways to continue:

- Begin with a gift. A self-hypnosis audio designed to help you become lighter in mind and body: www.beforeshewastamed.com/free

- Explore an evolving library of themed self-hypnosis audios: www.beforeshewastamed.com/collection

- Join the masterclass Be Lighter, a guided experience to help you embody the principles of this book: www.beforeshewastamed.com/masterclass

- Or claim your very own edition of before She Was Tamed - a return to yourself: www.beforeshewastamed.com/youredition

This is only the beginning.

Sources

kilder

This book contains direct hyperlinks to online sources in somewhat chronological order. Click the links for easy access.

All links are active as of November 23, 2025.

Find the full Viveura article I reference throughout the book here: https://www.viveura.com/archive/luxury-philosophy

https://thehappinessindex.com/blog/can-money-make-you-happy

https://worldpopulationreview.com/country-rankings/happiest-countries-in-the-world

https://www.sciencedirect.com/science/article/abs/pii/S2352250X22000550

https://seaglassrecoveryarizona.com/the-connection-between-dopamine-and-addiction

https://www.health.harvard.edu/staying-healthy/5-surprising-benefits-of-walking

Janice Bissex interview https://www.youtube.com/watch?v=pkJKmDVbBIY

https://www.jannabiswellness.com/resources

https://rockykanaka.com/sittingwithdogs

https://www.cdc.gov/nchs/products/databriefs/db283.html

https://www.buffalo.edu/news/releases/2009/03/9995.html

https://www.hopkinsmedicine.org/health/wellness-and-prevention/the-friend-who-keeps-you-young

https://www.bea.gov/data/special-topics/household-production

https://pmc.ncbi.nlm.nih.gov/articles/PMC7750273

https://news.northeastern.edu/2024/09/12/why-are-food-prices-so-high-price-gouging

https://pmc.ncbi.nlm.nih.gov/articles/PMC1115846

https://pubmed.ncbi.nlm.nih.gov/33112163

https://pmc.ncbi.nlm.nih.gov/articles/PMC1524969

https://pubmed.ncbi.nlm.nih.gov/33112163

https://pmc.ncbi.nlm.nih.gov/articles/PMC1524969

https://e-jmm.org/DOIx.php?id=10.6118%2Fjksm.2012.18.3.147

https://thepauselife.com/blogs/the-pause-blog/how-does-race-and-ethnicity-affect-your-menopause-experience?srsltid=AfmBOopRaowuxua1dWk-TKZDnB9Ka5oIpuy7XzHJjeN3lyVrsBvMYkM8q&utm

https://www.americanprogress.org/article/following-the-money-untangling-u-s-prescription-drug-financing

https://www.webmd.com/sleep-disorders/features/morning-light-better-sleep

https://www.energy.gov/energysaver/energy-saver?nrg_redirect=267583

https://www.energy.gov/energysaver/fall-and-winter-energy-saving-tips

Paris Paloma live https://www.youtube.com/watch?v=mMpro7fNLXo youtube.com

https://mcpress.mayoclinic.org/healthy-aging/the-power-of-neuroplasticity-how-your-brain-adapts-and-grows-as-you-age

https://www.theguardian.com/lifeandstyle/2025/feb/02/quiet-please-the-remarkable-power-of-silence-for-our-bodies-and-our-minds

https://www.thelancet.com/journals/lancet/article/PIIS0140-6736(13)61613-X/fulltext
https://wwnorton.com/books/The-Polyvagal-Theory

https://www.frontiersin.org/journals/psychology/articles/10.3389/fpsyg.2025.1539823/full

https://www.usda.gov/about-usda/news/blog/cost-raising-child

https://pure.au.dk/ws/portalfiles/portal/220344766/Anvendelseskritik_9_21_39.pdf

www.ingramcontent.com/pod-product-compliance
Lightning Source LLC
Chambersburg PA
CBHW021220130626
46554CB00004B/1291